Spirit Dances

The Best of Life

The stories shared in this book are about real people and composites of real people. The outcomes are true. Great care has been taken *to honor and protect* the actual identities of the people who inspired this book with the exception of my family and former husband who are included in all their glory. Where appropriate names and identifying information have been changed.

This book is designed to provide accurate and authoritative information with regard to the subject matter covered. It is sold with the understanding that the publisher is not engaged in rendering legal, accounting, psychological or other professional advice. If such advice or other expert assistance is required, the services of a qualified professional person should be sought.

Published by Sreenan Human Resources
P.O. Box 87
Ouray, CO 81427
www.melaney.com
coach@melaney.com

Publisher's Cataloging-in-Publication Data
Sreenan, Melaney
    Spirit dances : the best of life / Melaney Sreenan. —Ouray, CO: Sreenan Human Resources, 2003.

    p. ; cm.
    ISBN: 0-9729405-0-2

    1. Spirituality. 2. Spiritual life. 3. Self. 4. Meditation. I. Title.

B105.S64   2003   2003091992
204–dc22   0309

Project coordination by Jenkins Group, Inc. • www.bookpublishing.com
Interior design by Theresa Baehr

Printed in the United States of America
07 06 05 04 03 • 5 4 3 2 1

For all of God's nature and all of God's creatures

who have taught me to go inside and seek the truth.

ACKNOWLEDGMENTS

As I write these acknowledgments, I feel the strongest, brightest glow of dancing spirits around me. With endless lists of gratitude I deeply thank all of the friends, colleagues, clients, total strangers, and animals who will never know the influence you have had on me, and the wisdom and courage you have given me to go forward and attend to my highest dreams.

No heart has more gratitude than mine for the love and support of all I have been blessed with. For all of you that I do not name, please forgive me for I have a book full of you to thank.

I am grateful to my mother for teaching me the truth of life, self-discipline, and courage. I thank all of my siblings for being my friends and teachers along the path of knowing who I am. I thank Greg for his regular reminders of vision, Beth for her humor and wit, and Pat for consistent support. I thank Genne Boles for her everlasting essence, generosity, and never-ending honesty in her editing as well as her enthusiasm and support for Spirit Dances. She has been my biggest cheerleader. I thank Sage Morgan for being the knight in shining armor as the researcher on this project as well as a source of energy and enthusiasm that always kept me inspired. I am grateful in ways words cannot express for the friendship and support of Kathryn Koch, my personal assistant whose energy, organization and cheerfulness continually inspire me. I appreciate Linda and Howard Wiggs, Steve DePianta and Beverly Abbitt for a lifetime of friendship and always reminding me of my gifts. I thank Bruce Panter for his daily contact and for believing in me and helping me to keep the faith when I waivered.

I thank Tom White and the Jenkins Group for their guidance and knowledge. I thank Virginia McCullough and Jean Reynolds for their thorough editing and input on this project.

With heartloads of appreciation, I am grateful for the expertise, commitment and humor of Manny Schmidt and LINK Management International for their excellence in business marketing strategy development.

I am grateful to you, the reader, for wanting more from yourself and using this book as a guide. Please know that my loving, spirited support is with you.

Most of all I thank God and the Universe for giving me this opportunity to live a part of my vision to make a difference and for giving me my horse, Spirit Dances, for whom this book is named and who gave me lessons and experiences that keep on teaching me what life is all about from the core of who I am.

CONTENTS

INTRODUCTION

This book is inspired by my horse, Spirit Dances, a gallant black Warmblood, who came into my life as a colt. From the start, Spirit wore the look of a wise and playful child, and his every stride revealed the grace of a ballerina. Over the years, Spirit taught me important lessons about courage and creativity, as well as the value of persistence, power, and truth. Spirit, who moved forward fearlessly in every situation, taught me to embrace the dances of my heart that in turn have led me to the best of life's dances, which I call *"spirit dances."*

I wrote this book as a guide to help you unfold your own spirit dances. Since 1980, I have been working with people in the area of personal growth and development. I have been involved in corporate leadership development, including outdoor, experiential seminars as well as more typical indoor seminar formats. Along the way, I have learned that no matter where you go or what you do, ultimately, maintaining a sense of well-being always comes back to the issue of honoring who you are at your center and listening to what matters to your heart. After my seminars, people often ask me if I have a book or a guide to help them to grow in positive directions. When I have said that no, I haven't produced a book yet, the resounding response has been that I must get down to the business of writing one. Being a visual-tactile type of person, I appreciate that most people want something lasting to guide them, a tool they can look at and touch and work with on their own time. Thus, the seed for this book was planted.

I hope you will allow this book be a place to discover your spirit's true path, to provide a process through which you can make your wildest dreams come alive. Most important, I hope this book can help you learn to listen to the voice of your authentic self. So I invite you to take out your journal and accompany me on a journey filled with challenges and what I call "field play."

I designed this book as a journey of the heart. It can be a playful and inspirational read or, as I prefer, a more in depth nine-week or nine-month journey. You will need a very special journal, one that speaks to your heart. Take some time selecting a journal that is meaningful to you, as it is a very important piece of your Spirit Dances journey. As you select your journal consider its cover design, how it is bound, how it feels in your hands, and the color and size of its pages. Your journal should be very appealing and inviting to your spirit. Your journal will be used for many things, including answering specific questions in the "daily play." It will also be used for your weekly field play. Although many of the exercises in this book are part of a five-day seminar, as I organized this book I envisioned readers completing one chapter each week—in order. Each chapter builds on information presented in the previous one and forms the foundation for the next. This is an interactive program, and as such, I strongly encourage you to make this journey a major focus of your life for the next nine weeks. In other words, I urge you to make a commitment to your personal discovery journey. I promise you that if you work with the book's ideas and follow it's nine-week plan, you will come away with the truth about who you are, what you want, and where you are headed.

I invite you to discover your untapped energy, to unleash your truth of spirit, to listen to your intuition, to rely on the unlimited depths of your courage, and to tap into your innate wisdom. Let's dance, let's play, let's begin!

CHAPTER 1

LET SILENCE BE YOUR TEACHER

Spirit taught me that freedom expands the heart.

— MELANEY SREENAN, PH.D.

Spirit is waiting for you to rejoin her. She stands outside the boundaries you have imposed on yourself. There is no passion too great for her to contain; you will never be lost reaching for the infinite. She is the tenderest of infinities, whose only desire is to protect you and carry you in her arms from fear to love.

— DEEPAK CHOPRA

I have always equated silence with peace of mind and as a pathway to my spirit self. This self knows what it wants, where to go, how to be, and when to carry out its desires. Your spirit self doesn't know about limitations or deceit; it knows only honesty and is as sure-footed as my horse, Spirit Dances. At a critical point in my forties, I desperately wanted changes in my life, changes that only silence could bring to me.

For many years, I had attempted to bring silence into my life through meditation, yoga, camping, and various types of retreats. These initial efforts to bring silence into my life had great value, but I found I needed to access silence at a much deeper level. These early efforts with silence laid a wonderful foundation for the growth that was to come once I began fast-forwarding my life by giving up control and taking a leap of faith towards my future.

On November 1, 1997, a series of events propelled me to rethink my life and drew me into an intimate journey with silence that would eventually change my life. In the preceding year I had not only lost my father, my horse, and my dog, but I had also ended a ten-year marriage. These events had left me broken-hearted, disillusioned, and overwhelmed with self-doubt.

As I became silent, attempting to listen to my spirit self, the more my feelings of grief and loss became accentuated. Without question, my grief caused me to realize that my expectations of peace, happiness, connection, and success were in serious jeopardy. It was in silence that I realized I did not know what my spirit's definitions of peace, happiness, connection, and success were. My thoughts and the old definitions that had guided my life were a jumbled, fuzzy, unintelligible blur.

This lack of definition caused me to question my ability to do the private practice and corporate training work I loved and left me feeling dejected and heavy-hearted. It was time to heal, which meant going to the heart of my confusion to find some clarity. So I packed my car, and with my dog and cat as my only companions, I headed west. Since I felt like an earthquake victim with my life lying in shambles around me, I was grateful for the comforting soul energy my pets provided. As I sped away in my car in the gentle light of dawn, I was heartened that I was taking action to place my full focus on listening to my spirit's voice and to make a commitment to put its desires into operation.

This all sounds great, but the road I was about to follow was much bumpier than planned because over the next four months, it seemed the Universe's plan for me was much different from mine. I had told my colleagues and clients I was going to Sedona, Arizona, where I planned to spend four months rejuvenating. However, after arriving in Sedona, I realized it was not the place for me. Although beautiful, Sedona's barren landscape and desert surroundings did not speak to my spirit and I also felt overwhelmed by its mystical atmosphere. Listening to my intuition, I decided to continue on to Silverton, Colorado. Although I had to drive through my first snowstorm in the dark, over one of the most treacherous and avalanche-ridden highways in the world, Red Mountain Pass, I believed I had made the right decision to begin my quest with silence in the Rocky Mountains.

My ability to make my way to the discovery of silence in Silverton was supported by my resolve to focus my life on my authentic self, a self that was not based on being a "people pleaser." I had spent most of my life doing what mattered most to everyone but Melaney, and up until that day in November I had convinced myself that I loved my life. But that wasn't true. In fact, I never became accustomed to the heat and humidity and bug-ridden land of Florida; I had always longed for the mountains, with their distinct four seasons. In addition, I wanted to really get to know me, yet I was truly afraid of what I would find. What if I found a particular "me" I didn't even like? What would I do then? Still, somewhere deep inside I knew if I were to become a whole person, I needed to take some big, courageous steps. I believed that silence would fast-forward my growth process.

Inviting in the Silence

I planned to stay at the Silverton Dude Ranch, but when I arrived, my only welcome was a note from the owner. He wrote that because of the fierce cold weather he had taken his horses to the warmer climate of Louisiana for the winter. The note directed me to a 200 square foot space above the barn. This space had no radio, phone, TV, or any other link to the outside world, including mail service.

Wisdom is also developed through spiritual practice, for in silence you learn what can never be taught.

— FRANCES VAUGHN

That day, as I stepped out of my car, I shivered in sub-zero weather for I was still wearing my Florida overall shorts and hiking boots, which were working fine when I left Sedona. I was shivering in a silence that encased me like a cocoon. Even the snow fell silently. And paradoxically, the silence itself transformed into a loud, frightening, deafening, overwhelming force that screamed at me. But even amidst the fear the silence aroused, I could feel its pure, gentle, patient, nurturing presence calling me. It was the beginning of the quiet questioning and self-assessment that would clear the way to my spirit and allow me to discover how I wanted to live the rest of my life.

Through listening to my spirit in silence, I began to understand the difference between being a people pleaser and in making a positive difference in the way other people lived their lives. As a psychologist, my goal had been to help ease the psychic pain of my patients; as a coach and consultant, my goal had been to help my clients realize their true goals and potential. I now began to understand that the best way to do these things was by implementing the old adage of "being true to myself." Ironically, I now understood that I also needed to be an example of the courageous living I asked of my patients and clients. I could do so only by allowing my soul and heart to be the directors of my life. Over the course of about six years, I have learned to focus on what is important to me and to live for my soul's purpose rather than living to please others.

I also have learned to let go of the hectic life I had become so attached to out of fear and blind action. In my previous life, every minute was scheduled. I lived a hectic life trying to make time for everything. Every day I ran from one thing to another, from working out, then to my office, to community projects, and finally, back home. I'd practically dive into bed at night, all the while wondering where the day had gone. I would think about what it would take to add some space and some reason to my life. Everything was run by a "to do" list, including my weekends. I was living life as if it were a process of getting through it. This may sound familiar to you. I was getting through this day, this hard case, this trauma, this marital dysfunction, this financial dilemma, and on and on. It was hurry, hurry, hurry, with no time for depth of feeling, for reading a good book, for quality time with myself, for fun, or for authentic connection with others.

In living my purpose, I have come to know, nurture, and be with my spirit. I have learned to rely on not only my faith in myself, but also my faith in God.

Faith is....

When you have come to the edge of all the light you know,
And are about to step off into the darkness of the unknown,
Faith is knowing one of two things will happen:
There will be something solid to stand on, or you will be taught how to fly.

— ANONYMOUS

What Do I Mean by Spirit?

When I talk about spirit, I mean the great, wise guide we were each given at birth. Our spirit is the voice of the authentic self. In my hectic and noisy life in Florida, I ignored, disregarded, and doubted my spirit when it attempted to speak to me. I pushed my spirit away by staying busy, frantic, over-committed, and therefore overwhelmed and stressed. I drowned my spirit in a relationship that wasn't working, and I cut my spirit off by living in my head. I detached from the whole of who I was and became totally committed to "the rules," "the job," "the shoulds." I didn't listen to my heart. My spirit had been asking me to take a different path for many years, but the fear triggered by these requests was so great that it caused me to turn away from my spirit.

If we continue to repeat the same old ineffectual patterns, or greet each day with depression or frustration, it is possible we have deadened or silenced the spirit within. Spirit knows our deep, wise, uncensored truth. It is sometimes humorous or playful and sometimes serious or demanding. Think of your spirit as the intuition that God gave you. It speaks to you through your dreams and passions, as well as through your intuitive voice, which is best described as the gut level "knowing" that bubbles up to consciousness and advises you about your choices and actions, both big and small.

The great Sufi poet Rumi wrote: "Out beyond ideas of right and wrong, there is a field. I will meet you there." I have the sense that spirit reigns outside of all conflict and judgment and can be found in the space about which Rumi speaks. When I think of spirit, I think of my horse, Spirit Dances. I raised Spirit from a colt for five years and he died in 1995 from a mysterious cause. The night prior to becoming sick, Spirit got out of his pasture and had run for most of the night and, we suspected, ate something poisonous. Although Spirit fought hard to stay alive, he passed away after a week at the Veterinary Hospital in Gainesville, Florida. What I remember most about Spirit is that whether we were undertaking a tough dressage session or a relaxing trail ride through the woods, he always had a presence that came freely from his spirit. He emanated deep, wise, sometimes wild, and often innocent or playful energy. By his actions, Spirit demonstrated to me the existence of the untapped information that our spirits make available through the voice of our intuition.

Becoming aware that spirit has a great deal to offer to us is critical to the process we are working with in this book. Spirit had a direct line to my horse's spirit. I could see that he followed his instincts automatically, without thinking, without censoring. Whether it was an instinctual stop at attention to listen to his surroundings, or a passionate race with the wind, Spirit listened to the voices, the whispers, and the fleeting nudges of his spirit.

During my period of silence at the dude ranch, I became aware of the untapped information and referral sources I had available, if only I would stop and listen to my spirit in silence. We all have this information available, but we must be willing to listen. Once my spirit's voice broke through my resistance and made me aware of its presence, I had to offer my body and my mind as vehicles for living my spirit's truth. It took being alone, isolated at the closed-for-the-winter dude ranch in Silverton, for me to finally hear my spirit. It took the silence of being alone and cut off from the constant chatter of civilization. I had to ignore the admonitions of my colleagues who said closing my practice for four months was professional suicide. In trusting and having faith that my spirit would speak to me, I found the silence I needed to listen. And, as I stepped off into the darkness of the unknown, I was met with the solid foundation of my spirit and I began to fly.

The following essay was written by Author John Moorehead

The Paradox of Our Age

We have taller buildings but shorter tempers; wider freeways but narrower viewpoints; we spend more but have less; we buy more but enjoy it less; we have bigger houses and smaller families; more conveniences, yet less time; we have more degrees but less sense; more knowledge but less judgment; more experts, yet more problems; we have more gadgets but less satisfaction; more medicine, yet less wellness; we take more vitamins but see fewer results. We drink too much; smoke too much; spend too recklessly; laugh too little; drive too fast; get too angry too quickly; stay up too late; get up too tired; read too seldom; watch TV too much and pray too seldom.

We have multiplied our possessions, but reduced our values; we fly in faster planes to arrive there quicker, to do less and return sooner; we sign more contracts only to realize fewer profits; we talk too much; love too seldom and lie too often. We've learned how to make a living, but not a life; we've added years to life, not life to years. We've been all the way to the moon and back, but have trouble crossing the street to meet the new neighbor. We've conquered outer space, but not inner space; we've done larger things, but not better things; we've cleaned up the air, but polluted the soul; we've split the atom, but not our prejudice; we write more, but learn less; plan more, but accomplish less; we make faster planes, but longer lines; we learned to rush, but not to wait; we have more weapons, but less peace; higher incomes, but lower morals; more parties, but less fun; more food, but less appeasement; more acquaintances, but fewer friends; more effort, but less success. We build more computes to hold more information, to produce bigger problems; build larger factories that produce less. We've become long on quantity, but short on quality.

These are the times of fast food and slow digestion; tall men, but short character; steep in profits, but shallow relationships. These are times of world peach, but domestic warfare; more leisure and less fun; higher postage, but slower mail; more kinds of food, but less nutrition. These are days of two incomes, but more divorces; these are times of fancier houses, but broken homes. These are days of quick trips, disposable diapers, cartridge living, throw-away morality, on-night stands, overweight bodies and pills that do everything from cheer, to prevent, quiet or kill. It is a time when there is much in the show window and nothing in the stock room. Indeed, these are the times!

Do any of these ideas speak to your life? In thinking about the issues mentioned above, can you quickly address the questions they raise in your life? Please take out your journal now and allow 20 minutes to ponder some of them. Put your pen or pencil to the paper and just write the thoughts that come into your mind as you read the questions below:

• Have you pushed your personal boundaries out so far that you do not know where you begin and where you end?

• If all the things and possessions you believe you want appeared in your life right now, would you be happy?

• Do you believe more is better?

• Are you chasing after happiness instead of aligning your life around your spirit, with all of your actions oriented from that space?

• Are you asking what makes you happy from the inside out?

• What aligns your body, mind, and spirit?

• If your heart were to tell you what to do, what would it be?

I believe that true happiness, wholeness, and contentment prevail when we align the body, soul, heart, and mind, and that this alignment can be achieved by listening to our spirits. However, we must be still and quiet if we are to hear what spirit is telling us. Animals and children can be great teachers of the value of being quiet and in the moment; like a child sitting still on a porch or in a tree, simply gazing off to the land of dreams and imagination, or like a cat stretched out for hours, quietly looking out the window.

Watching Your Own Busy Life

Busyness is a way of silencing the soul. What does your busyness represent to you? What would others say about your busyness? When was the last time you were quiet enough to notice the little blessings around you? Have you noticed the way the clouds form pictures, or that little dogs are soft and comforting to touch? Can you note the way the sun catches a friend's hair at just the right second and makes it look like spun gold? Can you imagine how different your life might be if you practiced being quiet and still and not only began to see all the blessings around you, but also began to hear your spirit's voice?

Let's now examine how you are living your life. If someone were to follow you around with a video camera for a week and summarized your life, based on the video, would it be the life you want? Would you have been spending your hours and days doing the things you love the most, the things that arouse the most passion? Would the video show you spending your time and energy on the things that touch your heart and that you believe in? Would this "video life" have you fulfilling your values and your needs? Would you see yourself spending time with people you love, respect, and value and who love, respect, and value you?

In other words, would your video show you living a life balanced with the many things you value, such as your life's work, your family, personal care, play, and so forth? Ask yourself how you might feel after seeing a video of a typical week. Would you be happy for yourself? What might be missing? What values are you living by? Does this life match your deepest desires? Take out your journal, and answer these questions.

When I was in graduate school I started watching my life as if a movie camera followed me around. I didn't like what my movie played back for me, but I justified it by saying my life would be better "when"...when I finished my master's degree...when I didn't have to work and go to school at the same time...when I finished my Ph.D. program...when my student loans were paid off...when I bought a house...when I moved into my own office...and on and on. You get the picture. Things would be better when something else happened, and I had no conception of living in the present. I lived for the future and failed to find joy in the here and now. My videotape did not represent the person I truly was, what I actually needed, and the values that I wanted to live by. Although I was fulfilling many of my life's goals, I was not nurturing my spirit and living in a way that affirmed inner peace and joy. My videotape showed a person who loved the dramatic, had sleepless nights, was overwrought with family demands, had an excessive number of emergency calls from clients, had manipulative and controlling relationships, and was in marital and financial distress.

Through the process of being alone at the dude ranch, without intrusion from the outside world, while letting go of any firm ideas about what would become of my life, I was finally able to become still and quiet enough to hear the voice of my spirit. As I continued to listen to and to trust my spirit over the four months I was there, my body, which had been plagued with sleeplessness because of my racing mind, became calm and relaxed. The heaviness in my stomach disappeared and was replaced with a peaceful feeling. The tiredness I felt from constantly trying to swim against the flow of my spirit was replaced with energy as I plopped my inner tube of acceptance on the river and floated down the stream of my soul's desire. The silence was the teacher that allowed me to begin following my spirit's voice.

Summary

Life has so much to teach. It has so much to offer. I challenge you to summon the courage to hear the voice of silence and to let the whispers the soul speaks be heard as the chatter and noise you have created becomes still. As you listen to the wisdom that comes with this silence, you will begin to gather the strength to follow the words of your dancing spirit.

Spirit calls to you. She whispers sweet longings of your heart to you. She is summoning you to listen.

— Melaney Sreenan, Ph.D.

Meditation/CD

Take yourself off to a quiet place in your environment where you will not be disturbed for the next half-hour. Please have your journal nearby so you can write in it at the end of the meditation. When you are ready, turn your attention to your breathing. Just notice your breath and the movement in your abdomen as you breathe in and out. Just notice it. Imagine becoming more and more centered and quiet. Bring into this quiet space peace, calm, and tranquility. Surround yourself with joy. Imagine easing yourself into a special place all your own. You create this place. It can be anything you want. It can be on a soft raft floating on a calm lake, in a meadow in the summer, full of flowers and nature, in a room in a castle with light dancing all around, or anything you choose. Make this special place all your own. Fill it with all the things that give you comfort and peace and joy. Ease yourself more and more into this unique place. Maybe your place is a blanket of fresh fallen leaves, or a constant, salty, and warm ocean wave. Breathe in from your toes all the way to the tip of your head, out through your nose and back in again. Do this three or four times. Full, deep, warm safe breaths. With each breath, take yourself to a quieter and quieter space. Fall deeper and deeper into a state of quiet and of deep knowing. Breathe, hear your heart beat. Breathe slowly, gently, calmly. Allow yourself to feel as if you are held in a warm, loving, embracing light. Settle in more and more. Deeper and deeper. When you are really settled, ask your spirit what it most needs and wants. Listen for the answers from the deep quiet, from the wisest place within you. Listen from the garden in your mind. Listen from the soft ocean wave. Listen from the cool blanket of autumn leaves. Do not judge what you hear. Just listen. Listen without demanding it make sense. Listen, even if the answer seems odd or ridiculous. Breathe, open your heart, believe the truth will surface. Let go. Let the truth flow in. Spend some quiet time here. Breathe, trust, open, relax. Slow. Gentle. You. Listening, breathing, being. When you have all the information you need, thank your spirit and your special place for giving you what you need. Take anything you need from this place of yours and know that you can return here anytime. When you are ready, gently breathing, come back to this room, this time, this space. Slowly, very slowly become more aware of your surroundings. When you are ready, open your eyes. When you feel ready, write the answers that you received in meditation in your journal. What does your spirit need? What does your spirit want? Take whatever information you received and write it down in your journal. When you are finished, respond to the questions below.

Fieldplay

Answer these questions in your journal:

1. Who am I? Describe who you are without your roles and titles. (I am happy, peaceful, free-spirited, aligned with my heart, me.)

2. What do I want my life to be like? It may help to answer the question by listing the things you love to do and when you did them last.

3. Be the video camera of your life and answer these questions:

   • What are the positive and negative aspects of what I see?

   • List what you are willing to do to achieve the positive in your life and eliminate the negative.

   • How would I like my life to differ from the video?

   • What really matters to me? Why? Rank the importance of each item.

   • Who are the most important people in my life? Why? Rank the importance of each person.

   • What do I most like about myself?

   • What do I most dislike about myself?

   • How am I nurturing my spirit? (For example: Do you nurture your spirit by reading a good book, getting out in nature, spending time alone, or taking a personal development class?)

4. What generalizations, excuses and justifications have you made for not being aligned with your spirit? For example: I don't have time. I am too busy. I have too many obligations. I'll take care of me later. I'd feel guilty if I did something for myself. I'm not good enough.

Daily Play

1. Take four 30-second time outs each day and check in with your spirit and listen to what it wants and needs.

2. Sit quietly and clear your mind 20 minutes twice a day. As your mind brings words or images into your mind, acknowledge them and let them go, allowing your mind to enjoy the silence.

3. Once a week watch a child or animal play and notice how it reminds you of your spirit. Ask yourself how your life action is supported by your values. Ask yourself what resonates with your spirit. Ask yourself what in your life does not support your values and who you are.

4. Listen to this chapter's meditation twice a day during this week.

Resources

The Wooden Bowl: Simple Meditation for Everyday Life, Clark Strand; Hyperion, 1998.

> *Strand combines lively stories drawn from his personal experience as a teacher and Zen practitioner with short meditation exercises as he guides readers to use meditation to "be present to nature, to oneself, and to other people."*

How to Meditate: A Guide to Self-Discovery, Lawrence LeShan: Little Brown & Co, 1998.

> *An easy-to-follow and realistic approach that enables you to bring meditation effortlessly into your life, no matter how great the demands on your time.*

Simple Abundance: A Daybook of Comfort and Joy, Sarah Ban Breathnach; Warner Books, 1998.

A practical, inspirational daily guide that provides a meditation or exercise for every day of the year to help women pare down their lives and clear through their mental clutter.

The Laws of Spirit: A Tale of Transformation, Powerful Truths for Making Life Work, Dan Millman; H.J. Kramer, 1995.

A parable of a wise woman and laws of spirit, that help to make life work smoothly. A gentle reflection and spiritual education for all, the laws of spirit are at the basis of all religious traditions. Millman's outline documents their importance.

The Great Path of Awakening, Jamgon Kongtrul; Shambhala, 2000.

The classic guide to using the Mayhayana Buddhist slogans to tame the mind and awaken the heart.

Osho: The Science of Meditation
www.osho.com/homepage.htm
(212) 588-9888

Osho website is a bundle of wonderful information on meditation. An online shop and online audio about meditation and information on meditation resorts.

The Secret of the Shadow: The Power of Owning Your Shadow
Debbie Ford; Harper. San Francisco. December, 2002

The best book of it's kind on claiming the past and empowering the reader to a powerful future.

The Transcendental Meditation Program
www.tm.org
(888) 532-7686

The TM website offers program descriptions, a Q&A section, recommended books and a TM program locator database.

CHAPTER 2

DETERMINE YOUR DESIRES

Spirit taught me to give the impossible a chance.

— MELANEY SREENAN, PH.D.

When we are authentic, when we keep our spaces simple, simply beautiful living takes place.

— ALEXANDRA STODDARD

H ave you ever made a decision to do something for the wrong reasons?

Have you ever made a choice that intellectually looked and sounded right, at least at the moment, but at the same time part of you was rebelling against the decision? Have you ever made a choice that turned your stomach, brought tension to your shoulders, or just plain made you feel uneasy? These are all signs that you have just stepped out of your authentic self. If you follow an intellectual choice despite your body's response, you are probably functioning in a place that lacks internal integrity.

There are many ways that underlying self-deception can support a seemingly right decision. For example, marrying for money or security rather than love may indicate that the person is out of alignment with his or her authentic self. Likewise, choosing an easy career over one that provides challenge, or buying a status-symbol car that you can't afford are examples of actions that do not match the needs of the authentic self. Individuals sometimes join a certain crowd just to be popular or subscribe to an idea or philosophy that goes against the grain. They rationalize these actions because of some perceived gain, ultimately this can lead to becoming out of alignment with the authentic self.

I had a dear friend who loved the outdoors and absolutely adored nice things. She was a deep and wonderful person who was very loving, and outgoing, and gave consistent encouragement to her friends. She dreamed of living on a lake, driving a Mercedes, and having leisure time to sail, go on cruises, and vacation in exotic islands. When we were in college she excelled in the social sciences, but instead chose a major in marketing and sales because she knew she would be able to make much more money in the business world than in a career rooted in the social sciences. Although she was able to do well in the marketing, sales, and necessary math classes, she found no joy in them. These classes felt like drudgery, but she forced herself on and achieved the prized degree that would allow her to earn the money she needed to buy the material things she desired.

Money had always been an issue for my friend. She often spoke about growing up poor and vowed she would do whatever it took to live a life full of material riches. After college we took different paths but stayed in touch. She went to work in sales at an international company. During our conversations she went on and on about how much she hated her job, but she always added that she was so very successful. My friend also was very beautiful and knew her looks helped open doors for her. She got awards and bonuses for her hard work, but she still complained about the job itself. She said it made her chest ache and her heart feel heavy, but she liked the challenge and the money. And, she had her Mercedes and her grand vacations in the islands.

One day she called me and said she had breast cancer and she soon had a double mastectomy. My friend continued on her career path and remained happy with her material possessions and the lifestyle the work provided. However, she still did not like the content of her job—the actual work she had to do. She won a national award for being the top sales representative in the eastern United States and loved the glory and honor she received. My friend continued to complain about her lack of satisfaction and sense of fulfillment in her work.

Several years went by where we had very little contact. One day I received a phone call from her. She said she had lymphatic cancer, and was given three months to live. On her deathbed she said: "If I had just followed my heart like you did, I feel my life would have had true meaning. I gave my life to money, cars, nice things, and the company, and all I have to show for it is a plaque." The sadness was overwhelming and yet her insight was clear. The conflict inside of her for living her life from a place that was out of alignment with her spirit took her life, literally and figuratively.

No one truly knows the full range of the causes of cancer—and other diseases, too. While some illnesses can be seen metaphorically, and there is a mind-body connection, individuals should not blame themselves for every occurrence of disease. I do not know that my friend's cancer was the result of being out of alignment with her spirit, but I do believe that her life and death would have been more peaceful if she had listened to her spirit's voice throughout her life.

It was only in dying that my friend quieted herself enough to hear her spirit's voice, but it was too late for her to change her life and follow her passion. Even though she was still in her forties, her time on this earth was up, and she realized that she had traded true fulfillment for material things, which had not filled her with joy and satisfied her spirit's desire to use her many gifts. She had not lived her life with her body, mind, and spirit in alignment. Her mind had dominated her existence, and in doing so, her spirit became inaudible. She never realized her authentic self. I often think of my friend when I am contemplating stepping off the path of my truth.

Your authentic self awaits you, and you have to listen. In the noise and clatter of our lives, we often cannot hear our spirit's voice. We may live with fear of success, or we may live without making conscious choices, or we may live to please others, conceal our perceived inadequacies, or attempt to hide from pain.

How often have you heard yourself wish for more time, more money, or more fun? While these are normal and natural tendencies, I see people trying to accomplish them by racing off to "do" their lives. They are chasing after these things rather than experiencing the present. In order to be fulfilled, these individuals must slow down and be in their lives today. To enjoy peace and tranquility, they must be present in the moment as they walk their path. The simplest way of packing these attributes in your travel bag is by aligning yourself with your authentic self.

Many of us live by so many rules and "shoulds" that even when we do hear the voice of our spirit, we silence it. Are you living only from messages that your head sends you? Is your response to life mainly logical and strongly based in thinking? Or, do you allow your feelings and emotional intelligence to enter into the formula of decision-making about the way you live?

My mother has been one of my greatest teachers for taking risks and living from the heart. She has always allowed her higher self to direct her, even when everyone else was telling her she was "off her rocker." After my parents divorced, my mother was left with the responsibility for nine children, three girls and six boys, aged three-months to 16 years. She realized she needed more education in order to earn a living adequate to raise all nine of us. Fortunately, my mother loved learning and had already finished her master's degree, and in order to carry on her work, she needed to earn her Ph.D. She applied to Florida State University because she wanted us out of the cold, harsh Illinois winters. She was confident that she would be accepted and that we would all do well in Florida (despite our loud protests). She did the best she could to help us make the transition to Florida, including shipping our four horses ahead and allowing each of us to take one pet.

We pulled out of town in our ten-year old station wagon packed tightly with ten people and ten dogs, as well as pulling a horse trailer full of our belongings. In leaving Illinois, we left behind the security of a wonderful farm and traded it for the unknown of Florida. My mother was able to leave Illinois because she trusted the voice of her spirit and the desires of her heart. If my mother had tried to make sense of how everything was going to work out before she returned to school in Florida, she would never have managed to do it because none of it made sense. She made this transition to a new life because she, in following her dreams and intuition, was aligned with her spirit and the move felt right to her. Her decision came from her authentic self, reached through listening to her spirit. She came out of this decision with her Ph.D. in Clinical Psychology and well-adjusted, happy children. Her victory glowed brightly. She had made her decision from her heart with her body, mind, and spirit in alignment. She was living her truth.

Involving your heart center in your life in even small ways can make a positive difference in the outcome of your actions. For instance, if you choose to feed your body whatever is easy and fast so you can eat quickly and be on your way, what message is your body receiving? Is it perhaps a message that you don't care for it, you don't value it, and you don't have time for it? On the other hand, if you lovingly make yourself a nourishing, delicious meal, your body and mind become ecstatic and your spirit dances as you eat it. The love with which the meal has been prepared infuses the nutrients of the food and nourishes not only the body, but the mind and spirit, too.

A carefully prepared meal serves you on all levels. You are telling your body that you value it, care for it, and respect it. And because your body is also the home of your mind and spirit, they also feel blessed. Living from your heart center honors your whole being and opens your mind to guidance from your heart, spirit, and body.

Our Divine Design

I believe that if God wanted us to live from our heads She would have given us a head with legs and skipped the heart and gut part. Scientific studies have revealed that brain waves radiate out from the body only ten to twelve inches, while heart waves radiate out eight to twelve feet. Did you know that the brain basically receives information last, as much as eight seconds after the gut, our complex immune system mechanisms, and the heart? So why is it that we spend so much time in our heads? Is it because it seems safe to stay there?

Letting go of rational intellectual control and choosing to live one day at a time, embracing the belief that you are safe with a Divine presence Who takes care of you, allows your life to naturally evolve in accordance with your authenticity. Becoming clear about what you truly want in life allows you to live right now in a way that supports your authentic self.

Authenticity comes from the voice and feelings of the heart and spirit and from the internal "knowing" of the body and the mind. Authenticity goes by many names. We hear it called the higher self, spirit self, or real self, but by whatever name, you are living in alignment when you are deeply aware of your true values, your wants, and your needs. Many of us know all of these things and yet have reasons why they can't be acted upon. Authenticity cannot be achieved without courageously honoring the voice of our higher self.

What is Real?

The Skin Horse had lived longer in the nursery than any of the others. He was so old that his brown coat was bald in patches and showed the seam underneath, and most of the hairs in his tail had been pulled out to string bead necklaces. He was wise, for he had seen a long succession of mechanical toys arrive to boast and swagger, and by-an-by break their mainsprings and pass away, and he knew that they were only toys, and would never turn into anything else. For nursery magic is very strange and wonderful, and only those playthings that are old and wise and experienced like the Skin Horse understand all about it.

"What is REAL?" asked the Rabbit one day, when they were lying side by side near the nursery fender, before Nan came to tidy the room. "Does it mean having things that buzz inside you and a stick-out handle?"

"Real isn't how you are made," said the Skin Horse, "it's a thing that happens to you. When a child loves you for a long, long time, not just to play with, but REALLY loves you, then you become REAL."

"Does it hurt?" asked the Rabbit.

"Sometimes," said the Skin Horse, for he was always truthful. "When you are Real you don't mind being hurt."

"Does it happen all at once, like being wound up," he asked, "or bit by bit?"

"It doesn't happen all at once," said the Skin Horse. "You become. It takes a long time. That's why it doesn't often happen to people who break easily, or have sharp edges, or who have to be carefully kept. Generally by the time you are Real, most of your hair has been loved off, and your eyes drop out and you get loose in the joints and very shabby. But these things don't matter at all, because once you are Real you can't be ugly, except to people who don't understand."

"I suppose you are Real?" said the Rabbit. And then he wished he had not said it, for he thought the Skin Horse might be sensitive. But the Skin Horse only smiled.

"The Boy's Uncle made me Real," he said. "That was a great many years ago; but once you are Real you can't become unreal again. It lasts for always."

From The Velveteen Rabbit

— Margery Williams

Isn't it heartening to believe that once you become real, it lasts for always?

Examining Your Needs

What are your needs? We connect with our needs through our memories. To illustrate this, think of a powerful, memorable moment in the last year. For me it was cross-country skiing with my dog in the backcountry, where the air was fresh and new, the snow was crisp and glowing, and I was surrounded by the silence of nature. This memory illustrates my need to feel the presence of another being I love and who loves me, to be outdoors, to have time for solitude, to have time to exercise, and to be surrounded by nature's gift of whatever is quiet, fresh, crisp, and new.

You can also discover your needs by looking at unpleasant memories from the past. For example, let's say your sister had a godmother who bought her fancy party dresses for her birthday and holidays but she bought you a plain everyday dress. You might have grown up thinking that you were less important than other people and not worth the good things in life, such as pretty party dresses. You might, therefore, develop a need to either prove you were good enough for special things, or you might want to prove that you were not worthy of them. Either way, your true need has been distorted.

Examining Your Values

In order to live in authenticity, we need to be aware of the underlying values that form the guidelines by which our authentic self lives. Some values are universal and I believe it is important that all of us live by them. Love versus hate, honesty versus deceit, freedom versus control, integrity versus deception, kindness versus cruelty, compassion versus coldness, peace versus turmoil, harmony versus discord, balance versus obsession, generosity versus greed, and the intention of doing good versus evil are some examples. There was a time when I was not clear about my values. I would not let myself see the truth of my situation. When my life was chaotic, unhappy, overridden by crisis, drama, and busywork, it was endlessly tiring. I felt as if change was impossible, and when I attempted to change, contentment did not follow. Even though I came face to face with the fact that my marriage was over, and I acknowledged it, my life did not become better because I failed to act. I still was not living from a place that was in alignment with the values by which I wanted to live my life, and my life was simply a reflection of this.

In remedying this situation, I asked myself why I had been deceiving myself about my marriage. What payoff was I receiving from staying in the marriage? What payoff was I receiving for being totally overwhelmed and feeling rushed? As I asked myself these questions, I prayed for the insight and the knowledge that would keep me from repeating this self-defeating pattern. As I became quiet and listened, I began to see actions I needed to take to return to a place of integrity. When I realized that my lack of alignment was keeping me in a marriage that had been over for a long time, I decided to do something about it. As a result, my life began to move along a more authentic path. Life started to flow as I aligned myself with my values and authenticity. When you are clear about your needs and your values and begin to live by them, you are living with integrity.

The more inconsistent your message has been over time and the more you have created a tidal wave of chaos with your inconsistency, the clearer you must be about your needs and values, and the more patient you will have to be in authenticating your life. In changing my situation, I knew that if I truly wanted balance, peace, and harmony in my life, I had some serious work to do in proving it to my authentic self. Even after I faced the silence and became clear about what my needs and values were, the chaos still showed up in my life. The only way to avoid the chaos was to continue to choose my life based on my values and my authentic needs. Then, as I began to build a record of adhering to what I believed in, it became easier to choose the path that valued my authentic self. In some ways it was like throwing pebbles into a pond, creating those rings of disturbance that flow out from the point where the pebble hits the water. Each time I made a choice based on my values and my needs, it permeated the rest of my life, changing it in subtle but powerful ways. For example, in honoring my authentic self and ending my marriage, I found that the fatigue that had weighed heavily on me was no longer present and I became more energetic. As you align your values and needs with your authentic self, your confusion will end, too. This clear message of consistency must be sent to your authentic self through both your actions and your words.

When I speak of God, I am speaking of that higher intelligence that is called by many names—Creator, Mother Nature, the Universe, Buddha, the Divine, and so forth. By whatever name, God responds by giving you more of what your actions and words say you want. When my actions and words were chaotic, filled with drama and emergencies, God responded by giving me more of the same. When my message aligned with my values, it became one of integrity and created peace of mind. Wonderfully, God again responded by giving me more of the same. It is in the union of your body, mind and spirit that your life begins to be authentic.

Remember though, God responds when your actions are congruent with your words. When what you say you want and what you do are complete opposites, God goes with what you do. When the message you send is consistent with your authentic self, when your actions and words support this message, then God will respond with more of the same.

Learning and Growing

I believe the most important obligation we have in life is to learn and grow. What lessons have you had the opportunity to learn? Have you taken time in your busy life to address the lessons you need to learn? Do you find yourself repeating the same behavior again and again, in the hope that this time the *wound* in your heart will be healed? It is said that a sign of insanity is doing the same thing over and over again and expecting different results.

Is your life's energy drained from continuous failed attempts to create a life that fulfills your desires, dreams, and expectations?

To release yourself from this loop of defeat, you must find out who you really are. What truly has meaning for you? When you were six years old what made you laugh? What things did you love at age seven? If you had unlimited time, plenty of energy, a steady source of money, and no obligations, what would you do? What would your life look life without all the responsibilities you have gathered over the years? What if you were completely free to do anything your heart desired? What would that be?

Examining your childhood is a great way to learn more about who you are. It is also a wonderful place to discover what you authentically want from life. When you were a child, your family and your environment helped you to formulate rules to live by in order to be safe from harm and to make your way in the world. All little beings have special antennae that are constantly *feeling out* the environment around them to see what will make them acceptable to, and keep them in the good graces of, the people they depend on for their survival.

It is within our family of origin that we make the rules for our life and gain our perceptions of our place in relation to everyone else. It is within the family environment that we learn about the "enoughs" of life: good enough, smart enough, attractive enough, thin enough, fat enough, tall enough, short enough, funny enough, athletic enough, and so forth. We also learn the "hows": how to think, and how to feel in the way that is acceptable to our family, thereby learning what is expected of us. This also is the time that we disown parts of ourselves to avoid abandonment by our caretakers and protectors.

It is time to ask yourself if you believe you are good enough in that global, general way. What are your biggest fears and can you identify their root causes? What parts of your authentic self have you disowned in order to gain the approval, and thus to avoid the abandonment, of others? It is time to face your abandonment issues. Until the fear of abandonment is reckoned with, it will continue to disrupt your life. This is part of the human condition because on some level, we are all afraid of standing alone.

Take your journal and pen in hand as you contemplate the following questions and write down any answers that come to you. List ways that your abandonment issues:

- interfere with your relationships,

- stop you from taking risks,

- keep drama in your everyday life,

- stunt your growth and personal development,

- keep you holding back from your natural inclinations or holding on when it is time to let go.

Abandonment fears usually translate into creating limiting beliefs. Limiting beliefs are usually adopted as a way of coping with our desire to be accepted as well as a way to avoid abandonment. In order to protect our feelings—our hearts—we may have made up limiting beliefs about ourselves to avoid being hurt or harmed. Sometimes limiting beliefs give us the security we think we need to handle certain situations. By believing you are a poor conversationalist and avoiding parties, you are protecting yourself from the possible rejection by another guest taking offense to something you said.

As a psychologist who has worked with clients in a therapeutic setting, I have often observed that limiting beliefs often result from reactions or treatment received from parents, siblings, friends, teachers, ministers or other significant people encountered during childhood. Ideally, as teenagers and young adults, we review these ideas about ourselves and change the ones that don't align with our authentic selves. However, we often skip this process and show up as adults with irrational ideas about whom we are, what we are capable of, and about the world around us. Frequently these beliefs shape our lives, the relationships we form, and our expectations of what we can obtain from life.

It is no exaggeration to say that these limiting and negative beliefs own us unless we are willing to face them. For example, if we haven't examined our beliefs about intimate relationships, in the uncertainty of not knowing what we want, we may find ourselves marrying a person who mom or dad thinks is appropriate rather than someone who matches our authentic self.

Ironically, if you do not address limiting beliefs they often show up at the least expected and at the most awkward times, such as when you are on a date, taking an exam, making a presentation on a job, or being offered an opportunity. For example, when I was a teenager, my father divorced my mother. At the time of the divorce, he told me that I was just like my mother. Therefore, since he was divorcing my mother was he divorcing me too? Was I to accept the limiting belief that my father was divorcing his relationship with me? Was he divorcing who I was? He seemed so angry and upset with my mother all the time. Was he feeling angry and upset with me too? Was I unlovable, which was apparently the attitude he had about my mother? Make no mistake, I adored my mother, so how could he be so negative about her?

As I felt the pain of rejection deeply, and tried unsuccessfully to discuss it with my father, I ended up bearing the burden of the feelings aroused by the divorce—I took the divorce out on myself. I hated myself. I started telling myself that I wasn't lovable and I was stupid. The stupid part actually became one of my limiting beliefs especially when my father started telling me that I was stupid at age seven and encouraged me to marry young and depend on a man to take care of me.

A period of counseling allowed me to see my self-hatred and to begin to deal with it. Even so, it was a long, long time before I could lovingly face the person in the mirror. Lacking positive validation from my father, it was hard to find value in myself because I was convinced I was unlovable and stupid. Counseling also helped me work through the deep abandonment issues associated with my relationship with my father. As I began to heal I replaced the negative descriptions of unlovable and stupid with positive ones of loveable and smart. However, subtle layers of the rejection I received from my father still visit me at times. Usually these messages appear when I least expect them, but I face each layer as it comes and then give myself permission to hear the voice of my authentic self, who knows how loveable and smart I am. I then claim that truth.

I am not saying it is easy to overcome abandonment issues and the underlying relationship and intimacy issues that go along with them. However, I am saying it does get easier and better each time you face the issues and give yourself permission to hear and claim the truth from your authentic self. You are capable of complete, whole, unconditional love. The love that your authentic self gives you is always there to comfort and support you, if only you will listen to its voice.

What are Your "Tolerations?"

We all have things in our lives that steal our energy. These things can act like a leaking pipe that is hidden from sight inside the wall. You don't notice its constant drip, drip, drip until it saturates the wall, flows out, and quickly destroys your lovely wood floor. Now it has your total attention. The drip of the leaking pipe was tolerable while it stayed inside the wall, but it still quietly did its damage. It only became intolerable after the damage became obvious and there was no ignoring it.

Letting something remain unfinished when it needs to be addressed is considered to be a "toleration." (The late Thomas Leonard, who is the founder and former president of CoachU, a coach training and certifying university, coined this word.) A toleration could be a nagging stack of magazines you keep promising yourself you will sort. It could be that your car needs servicing or an errand you keep putting off. Tolerations can be big or small, but regardless of size, they steal your energy. When your energy is leaking out to myriad tolerations, it depletes energy reserves needed to accomplish the things that matter to you. You may feel too tired, too distracted, too overwhelmed, or just too disoriented to do the things that you really want to do. An easy way to look at tolerations is to think of them as the things in your life that tug at you, hold you back, and keep you stalled. Tolerations are things that you live with at some level, sometimes consciously in that they nag at you, or unconsciously, leaving you unaware that they steal your energy.

I remember when I was trying so hard to keep my marriage going. Due to the tolerations within this relationship, I was overlooking huge things. My energy was drained and chaos reigned. I had lost sight of my vision and my faith in having the life of my dreams. Holding on held me back and kept me in a cycle of accepting the unacceptable. Are you being held back? Is your past holding you back in the form of limiting beliefs in the present? Are old beliefs keeping you in bondage?

"...For at the end of the day, or at the end of a life, all we truly have is ourselves and love. And if we love ourselves - truly, madly, and deeply - all we have is all we'll ever need."

Something More

— SARAH BAN BREATHNACH

Summary

Dealing with your fears and past ghosts represents an important step in clearing the path for your authentic self—the real you. Beyond the chaos and confusion of your history is the deep and wise knowing of who you are, what you yearn for, and how to manifest it in your life by dancing with spirit.

Spirit dances with desire for the deepest most powerful you to join him. He longs for you to embrace the spirit in you and beyond.

— MELANEY SREENAN, PH.D.

Meditation/CD

Take a moment and close your eyes. Take a deep breath into being still. Slowly connect with the silence within you. Slowly, slowly, letting go and becoming more and more still and silent. When you are ready, find a safe and generous space in your mind's eye. It may be outdoors by a lake, inside an imaginary bubble or in the midst of a fantasy garden. When you have found this safe space, go there at your own pace. Go to this place that has the comfort and warmth and security you need to fall totally quiet and still. Take in a deep breath. Feel your breath as it fills your abdomen and upper chest. Breathe out slowly and deliberately. Feel your body relaxing up against the support you have put in place for this meditation. Quiet your mind... stillness... calm...slow... and gentle. See the sights of your special place. Experience the feelings within this safe place. Notice the surroundings of this secure place. Shift your attention to your authentic self. Bring in any light, energy, healing thought or feeling you need to as you bring yourself closer to your authentic self. Shift your attention now to the place where your authentic self is lost to the negative, mean part of you that shows up at the least opportune times. When you are completely relaxed and clear in mind, body and spirit, call forward the part of you, the gremlin in you, that doesn't want a thing to do with loving you or giving you credit. Feel the sensations of this energy, these thoughts and emotions in your body. Notice this in your heart, your head, your body. Where do you experience the most tension? How does the space outside of you feel? How do you feel as you look at your life, your relationships, your goals through the eyes of this negative, perhaps hateful, angry energy source within you? Focus all of your attention on this part that is so hard on you and let the feelings flow. Let all of the feelings and thoughts flow. You are likely to feel intense anger, blame, hate, and judgment. Let this internal conversation go uncensored. Stay with it. You may notice the negative voice gets quiet and withdraws. The dark side is less honest and prefers to come in the back door and surprise you or kick you when you are down. The dark side is afraid to be seen and is not motivated to be in the light. It has no desire to be out in the open. Your dark side knows it loses its power in the light. Allow yourself to exaggerate the power and words of this shadow aspect. Often it helps to be outrageous, determined to confront this part of you that defeats you, holds you back, and makes you crazy, confused, torn, and distracted from your highest self, this destructive part of you that keeps you from living from your values and needs. Address the part of you that has you living in the past with your abandonment fears, holding on, holding you back.

When you have completed this part of the conversation with yourself, slowly go back to the safe and wonderful space you have created for yourself and breathe deeply. Let go of this confrontation with the negative. The conversation may have been stressful. Just let it go now. Focus on the quietness of your breath and the security of this special place. Slowly and gently, breathe as you return to your special place. Reconnect with the loving, warm, comfortable feelings. Notice the freedom and the sounds and the safety in this special place. Breathe into the safety, and thank yourself for taking this time to go into the depth of your being and find the truth. Relax. Stay here until you feel complete relaxation and silence in your soul. Breathe peacefully until you are smiling inside and out. Be proud of the hard work you have done. Celebrate the clarity, the insights, and the discovery.

When you are ready, come back to the room and journal the things you have learned about your dark side in this meditation and describe the safe and generous space you created for yourself.

Fieldplay

Answer these questions in your journal:

1. Who are you when you are functioning in higher/spirit/authentic self?

2. What are the five strongest values you have? Rank them in order of importance.

3. What are the five strongest needs you have? Rank them in order of importance.

4. Are you in alignment with your five strongest values?

- In what areas are you not living from a place of alignment with these values?

- Where are you lying to yourself about something?

- How are you justifying a behavior that compromises one of your values?

- What important issue, that you are refusing to address, violates your values?

- How are you avoiding following the calling of your authentic self and all the power it offers you? For example, is your power drained because you continue to settle for a relationship or a job that isn't working for you?

5. How do you believe your abandonment issues interfere with your relationships, your growth and personal development, and your life in general?

6. What are the five top limiting beliefs you hold about yourself?

- Which one has the most power over you?

- Write it down and say it out loud in the mirror. For example, some common limiting beliefs are: I am not good enough...they wouldn't like me if... I can't...it's too hard...I don't know how...that's just the way I am... I am lazy... I am not smart enough.

Daily Play

1. List twenty things that take away your personal power or drain your energy.

2. What are you tolerating in your life?

3. What are you putting up with in your life that weighs on you? Continue to add to the list each day for a week. Then pick the top ten and resolve them.

Resources

The Life You Were Born to Live: A Guide to Finding Your Life Purpose, Dan Millman; Tiburon, CA: H.J. Kramer, 1993.

Designed to help you find new meaning, purpose and direction to your life.

Everyday Enlightenment: The Twelve Gateways to Personal Growth, Dan Millman; Warner Books, 1999.

Twelve keys to turning everyday life into a spiritual adventure.

Creating Miracles: Understanding the Experience of Divine Intervention, Carolyn Miller, Ph.D. Tiburon, CA:H.J. Kramer, 1995.

Ideas and principles, as well as true stories, for accessing the miracles in everyday life

Feelings Buried Alive Never Die, Karol K. Truman; Olympus Distributing. 1991.

A book that helps you know your feelings and grow beyond the ones that keep you stuck.

CHAPTER 3

SEEK A HIGHER WISDOM
AND LET GO

Spirit taught me that with trust you have it all.

— MELANEY SREENAN, PH.D.

"...I am bound to live by the light I have..."

— ABRAHAM LINCOLN

Life shrinks or expands in proportion to our courage.

— ANAIS NIN

I spent the winter in Colorado and then returned to Florida in March, 1998, but my heart longed for the cool mountain air. Even on a physical level, I missed Colorado's fresh, silent open spaces. My mind missed the freedom from noise and distraction that I had found there and my spirit longed for the freedom of being out in the Colorado wild. Although I was passionate about my work and loved my clients, something inside of me wished that all my business had gone away over my winter's retreat, and that I would have to start my life over. Of course, it followed that if I had to start over then I might as well do it in a place I adored and I continued to fantasize about moving to the mountains.

I was in Florida for only two weeks when I was overtaken with an all-consuming longing to return to Colorado, so the following month, I planned a trip to Ouray, a small mountain hamlet in southwest Colorado. I needed to see if there was a way to make a living in a town of less than 800 people and 360 miles away from Denver, the closest large city. My trip to Ouray ended up being both discouraging and unsuccessful. I was unable to discover a way to support myself in that area. I returned to Florida, having made the decision to settle for the next best thing, which was a resolve to take frequent trips to the southwest Colorado area. Still, these trips did not satisfy my longing to live there.

Months went by and in September 1998 I finally decided to make the leap of faith and just let go. Once I got there, I'd figure out my future one piece at a time. Abruptly, the demons of doubt began to rear their ugly heads. Moving to Ouray is crazy, impractical, and risky, these demons said. Why would I leave my family, friends, and the "perfect" work and lifestyle to begin my life again without a clue about what I would do to support myself? My beloved consulting business and private clients also tugged at me, becoming even more attractive and alluring. The perceived negatives of moving to Ouray began to haunt me. Surely I would get tired of the harsh, cold winters in a little town with no entertainment, no malls, and with seemingly no cultural activities for hundreds of miles around. Wouldn't I grow bored by the lack of people my age to associate with?

The resounding answer to my doubting questions was that none of my doubts seemed to be of any real importance. I could no longer ignore my higher self, and decided that I must follow my heart. Scared to the core and daunted by the obstacles, I remembered the words of Helen Keller: "Life is either a daring adventure or nothing."

I made a commitment to close my practice, stepping into faith and making the move. I knew it would take me a year to get my clients settled with other therapists, to turn my practice over to my favorite colleague, and to attend to the other details of organizing and downsizing. In actuality I am not a big risk taker, nor do I like change, but my heart was calling so strongly, I just had to follow it. The act of surrender, mixed with faith and conviction, helped to allay my biggest fear, lack of money. How would I make this work?

Once I had made the commitment to listen to the voice within and let go of my excuses, it was as if I had stepped onto an escalator that transported me from one miracle to another. Once I had made up my mind to move, spirit took over and made miracles happen. Three days after I became clear about what I wanted, my house sold sight unseen and for the asking price; and within a month my practice sold for the asking price. The house I wanted to rent in Colorado was available at half the rent I expected to pay and included utilities. Shares of stock I owned split, tripled in value, and I sold at exactly the right time. The miracles continued in every area. I received waves of support from every corner, including friends, family, and strangers. The support just kept coming to me. It was an overwhelming confirmation of my decision to follow my heart, affirm my value, and exercise my freedom.

Several months after arriving in Colorado, spirit rewarded me for my courage, and I contracted a job as a consulting psychologist for an outdoor, experiential consulting firm. How blissful! I was working outdoors, helping executives to change their own lives for the better and improve the atmosphere in their companies.

This chapter is about connecting with Higher Intelligence or Divine Presence or God, which simply put is the belief system that supports you in being the best person you can be. Ask yourself the following questions:

• Do guilt and fear drive your spiritual life?

• Do you go through the motions of doing spiritual work without implementing it in your life?

• Do you need to build a relationship with your higher self, God, the universe?

• If you felt fully supported by your God, how would your personality be different?

• Do you accept that your higher power is a loving, forgiving, and giving being that wants the best for you and from you?

• What spiritual beliefs support you in your life's path?

• Are these issues you need to address with your God through your minister, rabbi, or other spiritual advisor?

• Do you believe that addressing these concerns will clear your path and set you free to pursue your heart's passions?

Most of us have learned to either trust or not trust our higher power, but lack of trust can make the world a challenging place. Whether you come from one of the traditional faiths, such as Christianity, Judaism, Islam, Buddhism, Hinduism, or from a non-traditional faith such as a general belief in what you call the Universe or Mother Earth, a belief in a higher intelligence provides hope, energy, and direction. When we feel a deeper connection with something stronger and more powerful than we are, we can engage in conversations with this being or force, we can pray to it, and use it as a vehicle by which to face our humanness. This connection can form a solid foundation for the way we transport ourselves through life.

Prayer and Meditation

Do you have a way to fall silent, of clearing your spirit from all the worries of life? Is there a method you use to step back from your world? I recommend cultivating the spiritual practices of prayer or meditation. Having the ability to connect with the space beyond your immediate logical circumstances brings truth, perspective, and higher functioning.

Your meditation environment should please your spirit. Feng Shui, the Chinese art of placement and design, speaks to the importance of color and the arrangement of space. Your overall environment affects how you think and feel, and your meditation space is even more influential, so if this place is calm and beautiful, then the healing qualities are enhanced.

Evaluate Your Surroundings

Your overall environment is important, too. Answer these questions about your space:

• Are your surroundings full of distractions: dust, clutter, and things that need to be organized or tasks that have needed your attention for years?

• How do you think these distractions affect your inner being?

• If you like flowers, when was the last time you had some in your home or office? How much do you think your home and office environment affect how you feel and how you perform? Studies show that a pleasing environment provides a sense of well-being and improves performance. Even the colors in your office may influence your mood in both subtle and obvious ways.

I had a coaching client who ran a very profitable business out of his home. During our phone consultations he constantly complained about his lack of motivation and of feeling tired all of the time. Believing his environment might be the source of his problem, I asked him to get several housekeeping and interior design magazines and use the images to guide him in redesigning his business and personal space. Before our next session, he called to tell me that he had bought flowers for his office and home, and just that one change boosted his energy and enthusiasm and enabled him to complete a profitable project. Since then he has made more positive and nurturing changes in his environment and continues to maintain a weekly flower delivery. He no longer lacks motivation or energy because he has created a space that nourishes his spirit.

The places in which you spend your time must feed your senses, so become aware of what elements in your surroundings provide energy. This represents an important step in self-awareness, and when honored, can feed your sense of well-being. What if you were to change three things in your work environment and three things in your home to make them more pleasing to you? How would this step alter how you feel?

Be Clear About Your Intentions

Intentions are a big part of the "big picture" of your life. I think most of us have conscious intentions and unconscious intentions. Our unconscious intentions come from our life experiences, including the "scripts" we've received from others, traumatic events, and solutions that have helped us deal with difficulties or frightening experiences in the past. In our childhood and young adult years, unknown or unconscious intentions may have stopped the natural progression and maturation of conscious intentions.

For example, let's say that my conscious intention is to live my life fully from my highest self, and to live a life of being present and accepting of all I encounter. Let's also say that I have an unconscious intention to show the world that I am not the loser my family told me I was. In addition, I have learned from my religious training that suffering is good. Then my actual unconscious intentions are to put on a good show and be a good martyr. Do you see the conflict? Being present has to do with being secure in your sense of self. When you have this inner security and you like who you are, your ego's involvement in day-to-day life eases because you are at peace and self-contained. Others feel a calm, easy, validating acceptance in your presence.

Now the bad news: the intention to be present, which comes from your higher self, is automatically overridden by the unconscious or hidden intention. If you need to constantly prove yourself, then your ego will always focus on how you appear to others. You will monitor your actions from the outside, from the point of view of other people. You can tell when you are in this situation when you're asking yourself if you're saying the right thing or making yourself sound good, happy, and successful. Do I need to fix my posture? Do I need to brush the lock of hair hanging down my forehead into place? Are my clothes okay? Am I tall enough, thin enough, and do I look my age? Is my voice too loud? Do I appear smart?

The hidden intention takes on its own agenda and off it goes, saying, in effect: What about me? Tell me I'm great! Make me feel good about myself. Life is so hard, and yet look how well I do. Look how much I've suffered. I should be admired and looked up to for all I endure. The hidden intention becomes all about validating itself. This piece of unacknowledged intention can surface at the most intimate moment, causing an internal conflict between itself, the hidden intention, and the conscious intention. The agenda of the unconscious self is to get affirmation, attention, validation, and comfort. When the hidden self speaks over the higher self, people pick up on this incongruence and the messages you send are inconsistent. When you send this mixed message, the reaction of others may range from challenging the message to feeling awkward and discounting you as an individual. Or, they may pick up on your neediness and avoid you.

I had a coaching client who came to me because he felt rejection in every relationship he had. He reported being very loving, generous, and fun to be with. I could see how that was true, but I also glimpsed the mixed messages he sent. His generosity came with strings attached to it, and his love seemed like neediness, and the fun was a camouflage for a belief that he was unlikable and, therefore, he had to entertain others to make up for it. In other words, his generosity was interpreted as a need to please and as a way to compensate for his lack of confidence in himself. His love caused a negative reaction in healthy people because it felt like an attempt to manipulate and control them. As for his fun-loving nature, his unconscious intention was to hide his real self from others, to show them a good time, and to keep them from knowing the real person.

Synchronistically, I was able to gather some interesting insights into this client's behavior through talking with another client. She had just had a great date. The man she was with had flown them to a beach resort for dinner and then rented a boat to watch the sunset and enjoy the cool ocean breeze. As she described the evening, I made the connection that her date was the client I just referred to. When I asked her if she planned to go out with him again, she said no. While the evening was a lot of fun, all he talked about was how badly women had treated him and how women had rejected him since he was a teenager. His emptiness, martyrdom, and inability to live in the present were readily apparent to her. Unconsciously, his hidden intention to prove he was unlovable had set him up to be rejected once again.

If you find yourself in the same destructive pattern or unwanted scenario over and over again, then be aware that your unconscious intention may be running its agenda with or without your permission.

Choosing Your Focus

It's a truism that what you focus on is what will manifest. I remember a time when I went camping and kayaking with friends. It was raining when we arrived late in the day at our out-of-the-way place. I had visualized sleeping outside under the stars, not in a tent. As I struggled with whether or not I should put up my tent, the rain turned to light drizzle and I had my answer. I was to sleep beneath the stars as I had imagined, and I chose the dampness and freedom of being out in the open while others put up their tents and slept in dark, enclosed cocoons. I couldn't get over how the limitless and vel-vet-blackness of the night sky was lit up with an explosion of millions of brilliant stars at our 12,500-foot elevation. I was so focused on the beauty before my eyes and felt such awe in my surroundings that the rainy drizzle didn't even factor into my experience. I fell asleep with a big smile in my heart—and on my face.

In the morning, the difference between my experience and that of my companions became apparent. The night before, their focus had been on how late we arrived and how rainy it was. They complained about their tents and how the damp air made it feel even colder than the 30 degrees it was. They were concerned that the wet weather would continue throughout the week and ruin their experience. They went to sleep tense and frustrated and awoke stiff and tired. They suffered because of the focus they chose, which became apparent as they moaned about their aching backs and the hard, frozen ground.

My reality was much different from theirs. The overnight temperature had frozen the rainwater, and the artful display delighted me. The cold fall air felt fresh and crisp against my face. We were all in the same weather, under the same sky, at the same hour, at the same elevation, and yet our experiences were completely different. I expected to see mystery and beauty, and that's what I got. My focus on nature's wonders was wildly rewarded with the show of a lifetime, while their focus was rewarded with suffering and gloom.

Later in the morning, while kayaking and practicing rollovers and righting ourselves in fifty-degree water, we all got cold, including me. I started to focus on how cold I was and soon I began to shiver uncontrollably. "Melaney, you better get out of the water," my buddy said, "your lips are purple. You must be freezing." Agreeing, I made my way to shore with my teeth chattering. In looking back, I wonder how different my experience might have been had I focused on feeling warm and supported by the elements, rather than on being cold. I am convinced that the focus of our thoughts creates our experience, and that we shape our outcomes by the direction of our thinking.

Letting Go

Growing up I often heard the saying, "Let go, let God." When I felt as if I were swimming upstream to no avail, I would let go, and let God. Every time I let go of any perceived control over a situation, I would feel a sense of freedom and my tension would disappear. My shoulders relaxed because the weight they had been supporting was gone. My breathing would ease and my heartbeat became steady. During these times I would feel companionship, support, and a power bigger than me fill my life, and my struggle would fade. In childhood, innocence and trust made this exercise possible. Letting go gave me a sense of well-being. I really believed I would be okay, and everything would turn out all right.

Sometimes, even now, I catch myself promising to let go, but then I discover that I'm not really doing it. I can start the day with an intention to surrender to my Higher Power, but within two minutes I might catch myself back in the river swimming upstream, struggling again. In my work with coaching clients I would sometimes hand them a small towel and tell them to hold on with all their might, while I tugged and pulled and tried to wrestle it from them. When I asked them what they felt while they struggled to hang on, they might describe feeling tense, angry, frustrated, confused, tired, irritated, or just plain upset. Then I would point out that this little experiment parallels our lives when we refuse to let go. We grind our teeth, tighten our jaws, and hold our breath. In short, we struggle, and it's no surprise that we often get a less than optimal result. Forcing things, holding on, and holding back, all fit into the theme of trying to control our lives. These control techniques create struggle, and the outcome is usually mediocre at best.

Letting go is the opposite of the forced, the dramatic, the heat of battle. It is the opposite of pushing and driving to an end. Letting go is not giving up, however, as in rolling over and playing dead. Rather, letting go is stepping into your power and checking in with your intention. Letting go is realizing that there is a tug-of-war going on and then turning the situation over to your higher self and your higher knowing. Letting go means checking in with your goals, needs, and values and letting your authentic self run the show. Once you make sure everything is in alignment, you can then step back. Once you have done everything that is in your power to do, it is time to let go, to trust the process, and to allow the flow of your integrity and your power to take it from there. This is a journey that can start whenever you choose. It will continue to evolve as you practice and put awareness into it.

The Process of Believing

Believing means having faith that you deserve love, laughter, and joy. It also involves having faith in the possibility that you can become your best self and realize your dreams, desires, goals, and fantasies. Fostering the best in our lives includes believing:

- that you can be all that you want to be.

- in truth.

- in other people.

- in nature.

- that you will receive all that you want and need.

- in health, healing, and overall well-being.

- in the process of your life.

- in those you cherish.

- in the memory and music of your soul.

- that your heart's wishes and desires will be fulfilled.

- in the way of your path, including the necessity of challenges and changes along the way.

Belief is often found in the eyes of a child, a beloved pet, or an elderly loved one. They see the innocent truth as being so. By seeing through their eyes, we, too, may begin to learn what belief is.

Have you lost faith, stopped believing in dreams, people, truth, love, or the richness of life? Have you abandoned your beliefs because you have experienced difficulties on your path? Have you stopped pursuing the things you once held fast? Have you abandoned your wants, dreams, and fantasies because of others' opinions? Perhaps you have begun to trick yourself into thinking such things as, "Oh, those are just immature longings," or, "I was just being idealistic."

Having faith and holding beliefs are intrinsic parts of the whole of life. Without faith, important components of your basic drives—your spirit and intuition—detach or splinter off from the rest of your being. We are all here for a reason, and it is our responsibility to believe in ourselves and find the courage to live our individual journey with authenticity and integrity.

We create our destiny by what we believe. When we do not believe we are worthy of our spirit's passions, we unconsciously play those negative beliefs over and over in our minds, and without even knowing it, we have hypnotized ourselves into mediocrity and acceptance of the mundane.

In essence, our negative beliefs distance us from our authentic selves. If negative beliefs are ruling your life, it is time to go on a treasure hunt to find the positive, glowing beliefs shining out from your spirit. They wait for you behind the clouds caused by your negative beliefs. Try to remember the idealistic ways you looked at things when you were a child, and perhaps during your adolescence. Where have those positive elements of your essential spirit gone? Have you reviewed your childhood to try to reacquaint yourself with the beliefs that existed way back when?

From early childhood until we went off to different colleges, I tagged along with my older brother Greg. Greg believed in himself and set a good example. He always believed in the truth of things and held fast to the idea that he could make his dreams become a reality simply by believing in them. More than anything, he loved to fly planes, and to everyone's amazement except his, Greg had his pilot's license before he had his driver's license. You see, he believed.

Greg also believed in alleviating suffering when a tragedy occurred and he wanted to use his love of flying to help people. He combined his love for the law with his love for flying and became an aeronautical attorney. As a college student, when he talked about his dreams, I thought he was being unrealistic. This was not the case. His beliefs were a powerful force that would not be stopped. His spirit, his heart, and his authentic self were aligned behind him. Through this alignment, his faith in his vision and a lot of hard work, his deepest desires became a reality.

Life is waiting for you to grab hold of your intention, to focus on your dreams, to believe in your Divine intelligence, and to step into letting go. You can do it! You belong to your truth and your higher knowing. Spirit will guide you.

Summary

Prayer, meditation and connection with the heart self is where truth, higher functioning, and completeness reign. Your dancing spirit knows the way of the warrior within. Intention must live in faith and in the process of letting go.

Spirit invites your trust to unfold as you enter the place of higher wisdom. She is dancing with the hope of joining you in this space.

— MELANEY SREENAN, PH.D.

Meditation/CD

Find your quiet space and settle in. You can either lie down with your spine straight or sit with a straight spine. Imagine being totally relaxed and calm, going deeper and deeper into the stillness and quiet. Feel your body, mind, and spirit relax and flow into nothingness. Find yourself becoming more and more peaceful. Let go of any thoughts that come to your mind, as if they were clouds floating across the sky. Breathe slowly from the deepest part of your being, hold the breath, and then slowly and deliberately breathe it out. Your breath is going in and out, you are breathing fully and completely. Breathe in this deep way three or more times. Now as you breathe slowly, scan your body for any tension or anxiety. Breathe into it and as you breathe out, let it go. Breathe into that space and let go even more. Deeper and deeper...letting go more and more. Gently, when you are ready, go back to a time in your life where you felt completely nurtured and cared for. Who was there? What did it feel like to you? What mattered most to you about this time? Now go to a time in your life when you didn't feel safe and see where you feel it in your body and mind. Who was there and what was the strongest feeling. What did you do to cope with this feeling or this event? What promise did you make to yourself during this event? For example, I'll never volunteer my opinion again. I'll never try that again. People are mean; I'll protect myself from them. What beliefs did you make about yourself and others? I am stupid, helpless, incompetent? No one loves me, wants me, believes in me? Who do I trust now? Do I trust myself? How have this memory and other similar events influenced my intentions, faith, focus and other life choices? What is the common thread that runs through all of these memories? Find a common theme. Stay in this safe and gentle place and just see what comes up. Ask the question to your heart and then trust the answer that comes back to you. Breathe in all the comfort and ease you need to stay with this question until you get the answer. Gentle...loving...flowing. Ask yourself and listen with love. Ask your wisest self to guide you to the answer to the questions about trust. How do I trust? Do I trust? Ask and listen. Ask and listen some more. Patiently stay in this space until you have the answers. Do not try to make sense out of them. Just trust that your *wise spirit will clarify for you. Check in with your breath. Thank your guide for the answers you have received. When you are ready, begin to come back to the here and now slowly. At your own pace, gently come back to this room and this time and place. When you are ready answer the questions in fieldplay.*

Fieldplay

Questions to answer in your journal:

1. Who do you trust? Who do you completely and fully trust? Do you trust yourself to take care of you? On a scale of 1-10, how much do you trust yourself?

2. What is your biggest obstacle to having a regular prayer/meditation time? If you have a spiritual practice what do you most need to do to take it to the next level? How will you and your life be different if you take this step?

3. What does your higher self desire? Write it down!

4. What do your ideal meditation, home, and work areas look like? List three important things for each area, and then make these necessary changes.

5. What has been your main focus in life? What does your major focus need to be for the next three months? For example: being your own life coach, improving your health, or rethinking your career?

6. What beliefs or ideas have you given up on? What has made you give them up? No time? Not enough money? No support? Lost hope?

7. What are the top five damaging beliefs you need to let go of? What are the top five positive beliefs that you need to put into your life? How will you be different if you do this? Happier, more outgoing, more genuine?

Daily Play

1. Listen to what your higher self is asking for. Write it down.

2. Create your ideal meditation space to use daily.

3. Look at your list of values daily, and answer these questions:

   • How is your daily life action supported by your values?

   • What in your life today really resonates for you?

   • What in your life today does not support your values and who you are?

Resources

The Way of the Peaceful Warrior: A Book That Changes Lives, Dan Millman; Starseed Press, 1984.

> *This bestseller is based on the story of a champion gymnast who, guided by a powerful old warrior, journeys into realms of romance and magic.*

Sacred Journey of the Peaceful Warrior, Dan Millman; Starseed Press, 1991.

> *The author provides readers with perennial wisdom and guidance for life, as he shares his adventures on the first steps of his sacred journey.*

Between Heaven and Earth, Marriet Beinfield, L.Ac. and Efrem Korngold, L.Ac., O.M.D; Ballantine Books, 1991.

> *A guide to who you are through the principles of Chinese medicine.*

Divine Guidance. The Secret Way to An Abundant Life, Jerry Overton Ph.D.; XLIB-RIS Corporation 2001.

> *Necessary understanding and principles for having the life you desire using the Divine.*

Conversations with God, Neale Donald Walsh; Hampton Roads Publishing, 1995.

> *Walsh has written several books in this series. Inspirational and insightful dialogue from God through Neale.*

Spiritual Madness: The Necessity of Meeting God in Darkness, Caroline Myss; Audiotape, 2 cassettes: Sounds True, Boulder, CO, 1997.

> *Assisting you in clarifying your spiritual self.*

Soulful Living.com
www.soulfulliving.com
(310) 287-0865

> *Soulful Living provides information on valuable books and audiocassettes, a monthly column for your soul, and great links to other sites promoting a peaceful way of life. This is a wonderful site.*

The Right Questions, Ten Essential Questions to Guide You to an Extraordinary Life, Debbie Ford; Harper San Fransico, 2003.

CHAPTER 4

BUILD YOUR CHARACTER

Spirit taught me to treasure the precious in everything.

— MELANEY SREENAN, PH.D.

In following dreams, destiny is found.

— JODY BERGSMA

B eing your genuine self is contingent upon knowing who you are and creates the pathways that lead to living the life of your dreams. So, who are you? I posed that question in Chapter 1. Did you take time to answer it? If not, please take a minute now to go back to the first chapter and answer that question.

When I refer to being your genuine self, I mean being comfortable with all of who you are, that is, knowing and accepting all parts of yourself. Being genuine requires doing a personal inventory each day, which means assessing the values by which you are living. This inventory allows the truth of who you are to shine through in your daily actions and deeds. Being genuine requires that you achieve a certain comfort level with your imperfections. In essence, it means coming to terms with the parts of yourself that you don't want the world to see.

Our imperfections lead us to be super-sensitive or super-*in*sensitive in our dealings with others and when we are honest about it, we begin to understand that this imperfect part isn't so tough and strong after all. All of us need to acknowledge the part of us that is a strict perfectionist and leads us to be hard on ourselves, as well as hard on those to whom we are close. Our job is to let that part go, including the unforgiving and judgmental self-talk that turns on others, too. When we are genuine individuals we know all about the perfectionist and we make peace with it while maintaining boundaries around it.

I have self-talk that says, "You know Melaney, you really don't have anything special to offer." In order to be genuine, each time I begin to write or present a seminar I must have a conversation with my perfectionist. I set rules and limits, and then I get agreements from the parts of me that are still growing and changing to give me a break—just let me be. These dysfunctional voices come from traumatic childhood experiences. At times, some of the voices have immobilized me; some still would if I had not acknowledged them, shown them some consideration, and then integrated that aspect of myself into my being. It is in owning these voices, acknowledging them, and having conversations with them that they lose their power over you and give you the freedom to show up fully you.

The Authentic, Genuine You

Attempting to love and accept yourself fully often stirs up a great deal of resistance. For many, it triggers negative thoughts. However, self-love involves considering the whole of your being when you make choices, thereby ensuring that they serve your highest good, and, therefore, the highest good of all those that come in contact with you. Rather than making you self-centered, true self-love makes those around you feel at ease, blessed, and honored because true self-love is outer-directed and allows you to meet each others' wants and needs. Healthy self-love is not an egocentric love like that of two-year-olds who focus exclusively on what they want and have little consideration for everyone else.

Healthy self-regard is genuine, authentic, and grounded in knowledge about what you want and need. This kind of love operates in the world in positive ways within your value system. When you experience healthy self-love, you feel calm, peaceful, happy, and joyful. You know it when you feel it because it is so right. You exude clear energy that others can see by the way you communicate. Your energy puts those around you at ease, which allows their genuine self to surface.

In short, self-love encourages growth and is contagious. This kind of love allows you to see the good in yourself and to acknowledge all that you have already accomplished. In addition, loving yourself fully and completely involves having your needs met automatically because you have educated the Universe, your surroundings, and all the beings within it (i.e., pets, friends, colleagues, bosses, clerks, and children) about what you need. A healthy relationship with yourself provides an internal platform for having the life of your dreams, the relationships of your highest fantasy, and abundance and joy.

Principles to Build Genuine Character

Use the principles below as your guide to examine and strengthen your genuine self.

1. LOVE YOURSELF FULLY.

This idea often stirs up great resistance. For many people it conjures up thoughts of being self-centered, conceited or stuck on themselves, but the truly self-centered must have everything their way to the exclusion of others' needs and desires. Truly self-centered people act superior to others and many are preoccupied with their looks. These individuals often demand to be the center of attention and they choose their associations with others based on what they can offer them. Usually no room exists for sharing or having a two-way relationship.

Ironically, many of us are afraid that if we love ourselves fully, we will end up like these self-centered folks. However, the opposite is true. In actuality, conceited, self-centered individuals do not like themselves. A conceited attitude is a cover up for, "I don't like myself" and self-centered behavior compensates for not feeling good enough. Often quite needy, these people drain others and go from one relationship to another. So, if you do not love yourself, you are on the road to the dreaded world of the self-centered and egotistical.

When my clients resist making peace with the things they do not like about themselves and have difficulty with self-love, I often say, "If God loves you unconditionally, what gives you the right to pick yourself apart?" Self-acceptance is a necessary ingredient for self-love and in turn, self-love is an important ingredient in developing strong personal character and what I call "psychological backbone."

2. YOU CANNOT GIVE WHAT YOU DO NOT HAVE.

I cannot give love if I do not have love within me. The summer I was 14, I saw a counselor and worked through some hurt and confusion in my relationship with my father. At the end of the summer, as I ended my last session with my counselor, he said, "You know, Melaney, if you do not love yourself, you will never be able to love someone else." At the time, I thought, "What a crock. I love my brothers and sisters, and I would give them the shirt off my back. Why do I have to love myself?"

For a while, I set out to prove the counselor wrong, but I found that each time I tried to love another without loving myself, I was disappointed in the outcome. So, the counselor was right after all and self-love was what my relationships lacked. Without self-love, the delivery and tone, along with the depth and meaning of my words and actions, did not convey what I intended. As I learned to love myself, I gradually began to realize what the counselor meant. As self-love grew, the love I offered to others was received in a more satisfying way. This happened because my inner strength had grown and reinforced everything around me.

If in doing a personal inventory you find yourself lacking self-love, then now is the time to discover why this is the case. Not that self-love is easy. In fact, it can be one of the most difficult things you'll ever do. The process still challenges me. But remember that self-love can be measured in levels, like rungs of a ladder. In the beginning it may be only an inkling that carries the internal "volume" of a whisper.

So, what will it take for you to move up the ladder of self-love? It is important to think about what you hold against yourself in order to justify the lack of self-love. For many of us it involves an inability to forgive ourselves for an action or behavior we regret or something we did that violated our values. In simple terms we have trouble getting past feelings of shame. It's as if we hold a grudge against ourselves and the guilt piles on, which then leads to self-punishing behaviors and attitudes. We often engage in self-punishment by treating ourselves poorly. For example, we may convince ourselves we do not deserve to have the relationship or career we really want. Remember that we can't give what we don't have in the first place. This stumbling block in moving forward often can be traced back to lack of self-forgiveness.

Examining this area of guilt and punishment may be the hardest, yet most necessary, step you can take. You may need to pray, or talk to a friend, a coach, or a counselor to get more clarity about what past issues continue to hold you back. And I invite you to trust that you have all the answers within you.

3. STOP THE SELF-DEFEATING THINKING AND BEHAVIOR.

Your psychological backbone depends on your determination to stay in your own corner and strive to bring out the best within you. Negative self-talk must go. Continuing behaviors that you are ashamed of demoralize your spirit. For example, if you are a closet smoker or use language not becoming to your psyche or self-image, supporting your genuine character will be a struggle. But self-defeating behavior is difficult to overcome if you don't know the root cause of it. You may need to review your history to determine what drives the behavior. Sometimes it's just a bad habit that needs to go. Taking a personal inventory will enable you to let go of the negative energy feeding the self-defeating behavior. I recommend that you examine what drives any negative habit or behavior, and then commit to confronting the behaviors because they no longer serve your life.

4. FOCUS ON YOUR STRENGTHS.

You are a wonderful and unique human being and it is your job to honor your special wonder and beauty. As you honor your gifts, you create a higher vibration in your body, mind, and spirit. And good energy begets more good energy. You radiate love and acceptance when you honor your strengths. Focusing on your good qualities builds confidence and opens the heart. Your psychological backbone stands proud and tall when you are filled with loving and confident energy.

Cultivate Self-respect

Self-respect is imperative to living a fulfilling life. Think about what self-respect means to you. Is it driving a fancy car? Wearing a lot of jewelry? Being able to tell someone off? Going after material things and aggressive and defensive behaviors represent signs that self-respect is lacking. As I define it, self-respect means upholding and honoring your true self.

Some people value peace and tranquility, but these qualities are illusive and missing much of the time. But in order to have peace in your life, you must also have self-respect, a component of which is the ability to love yourself fully and unconditionally. Seventy-five percent of peace comes from within and grows from gratitude, forgiveness, and holding on to faith in yourself, which is what self-respect is all about.

Self-respect shows. Others usually can see if you are treating yourself fairly, honestly, and lovingly. You can clearly see if what you truly want becomes available to you without effort. You attract what you want by your attitudes, beliefs, and behavior. For example, self-respect leaves you open to constantly attract moments of peace, happiness, fulfillment, and joy.

By the time we enter adulthood, many of us habitually say awful things to ourselves. It's such a firmly entrenched habit that we are no longer aware of the way these insults undermine and limit us. Become aware of the scripts that run through your head. When my clients listen to the uncensored critic, they catch it saying such things as:

You're:

- *dumb*

- *stupid*

- *ugly*

- *crazy*

- *lazy*

- *worthless*

These silent tapes can be very powerful and you may catch them playing over familiar phrases:

- You'll never amount to anything.

- You can't do that.

- You'll always need someone to take care of you.

- You'll never be good enough.

- You'll never be smart enough.

- You'll never be thin enough.

- You can't make it on your own.

Do any of these statements sound familiar? These disrespectful mental tapes usually come from people who ultimately form important parts of our personal history. Teachers, peers, parents, siblings, grandparents, dance or piano instructors, and coaches can plant negative seeds that become part of a tape that plays in your head. Complete strangers may make a remark or behave in a way that damages your self-image, and your own imagined fears may fuel the tape.

My dad "appears" on one of my parent tapes. A successful attorney, he undermined my confidence when I struggled with math homework. "Relax, sweetheart," he'd say, "you can be a secretary and some rich attorney will come along and marry you and you will never have to worry." My father probably meant well, but I felt put down and angry. The message I received was "you can't make it on your own." I rebelled against his message of dependency. Instead, his message inspired me to live an independent lifestyle.

Before he died, I playfully reminded him of the things he said. He had a hard time remembering those statements. "I do remember worrying about you because you were so sensitive," he once told me. "I was afraid you couldn't make it in the cold, cruel world." In looking back, we could laugh at his fears because I was able to become financially independent by the age of 16. My main source of income was training, showing, breeding, and selling horses and dogs, which I began doing at the young age of eight. Because of this business, I completed undergraduate work, earned a master's degree, and went on for my doctorate without my father's financial assistance. By the time my father and I were able to discuss his past doubts about me, I was a college professor with a successful private practice and he easily saw that I could truly make it on my own.

In order to gain self-respect, it is necessary that you know how you *want* to feel about yourself. Then identify the negative tapes from the past that play in your head and sabotage self-respect and self-love. Finally, you must work to consciously and consistently confront and overcome those self-defeating thoughts.

Cultivating Self-Esteem

How would you describe yourself? How do you honor yourself? In other words, do you hold yourself in high esteem? What you say to yourself, or what you think others believe about you, influences you and those around you. These thoughts and beliefs have a huge impact on your life. Think of this impact on a scale of one to ten. When you are young the impact others have on you is a ten. When you are mature the impact others have on you can still be as strong as an eight or more.

You may remember a research project that studied a large number of children from varying environments and having different levels of IQ. The children with reportedly high intelligence were put in a classroom where the instructor was told that the children were slow learners. Then they put the children who were not considered smart in another classroom and told the instructor that her students were very intelligent children. As you can predict, the instructors treated the children accordingly, expecting little from the supposedly low IQ children and requiring a great deal from the reportedly high IQ children. The children responded to expectations. When the teacher *expected* them to be smart they performed very well, but the children who were not expected to be smart behaved in accordance with low expectations and performed poorly.

This study, along with numerous others, demonstrates that how we are treated, especially as young children, absolutely influences our success, our self-esteem, our choices, and sets the stage for what we believe about ourselves. However, to live fully we need to understand that as adults we have control over the beliefs and feelings that we direct towards ourselves, and which, subsequently, strongly influence the way others treat us.

Without question, self-evaluation influences everything you do. Think for a minute about your relationship choices, remembering that people get their cues about how to treat you from both verbal and nonverbal communication. For example, folding your arms across your chest and crossing your legs sends the message: leave me alone. In that case, your nonverbal communication shuts people out. Perhaps your inner critic is running rampant and is afraid to open up, but you're not aware of it. However, other people, especially those closest to us, know that our crossed arms or other back-off postures may mean that we could be struggling with dramatic self-defeating thoughts or we are oblivious of our own non-verbal behavior.

Perhaps you give yourself a disgusted look when you pass by a mirror or you make a self-deprecating comment when you behave in a certain way but expected something different from yourself. What is communicated with this negativity? Not making eye contact with others also shows lack of self-respect and suggests you lack self-confidence. Do not despair if you catch yourself in these self-defeating behaviors. Self-esteem often begins to improve if you have a strong and active intention to change your self-talk. Remember the words from the children's story, *The Little Engine That Could*: I think I can...I think I can...I think I can.

Strengths and Weaknesses

In both my corporate and personal development seminars I include a section about listing strengths and limitations. Most participants can easily run off the list of weaknesses and may take twice as long to write them down as they take to list the same number of strengths—and they struggle the whole time. Of course it's important to identify your weak points, but to give them a more prominent place than your strengths damages self-esteem.

Self-esteem and self-respect are related, and one nurtures the other; however, this happens only if the underlying self-talk is positive. Self-respect is the product of the healthy self-esteem that you achieve through positive thoughts of and conversations with yourself. (Yes, you can talk to yourself, just don't tell anyone I said so.) Think of this as a continuous loop: positive self-talk leads to positive self-esteem and, therefore, to self-respect.

Honoring Your Unique Nature—Your Preciousness

Self-love includes acknowledging the precious being within you and owning your unique and wonderful nature. I believe we are all precious beings of God. That within all of us is the preciousness of a child, the uniqueness of nature, and the beauty and grace of an angel. Do you have people around you who value your preciousness and who honor your unique nature? Preciousness is part of the mystery of life, the indefinable essence that is you. It is the preciousness a lover sees when he or she falls in love. It is the preciousness a loving mother feels the first time she holds her newborn. Preciousness can be seen in your God-given joy, innocence, and bliss. It is the purest form of you. It is you with the layers of defenses, adaptations, coping mechanisms, and facades all stripped away.

I had the honor of watching the birth of my horse Spirit Dances and I can still feel my elation when he arrived. His preciousness was pure and so innocent. He had no fears, defenses, or worries, and exhausted by all the stimulation around him, he sat down in my lap. As I sat on the floor in the stall with Spirit Dances, I was touched that he was undefended and undefined, trusting and worthy. The experience will last for a lifetime. He didn't do anything to bring about this experience; rather, it came about through his being—his fully authentic, innocent, purely "spirit dances" being.

So, if you were to see yourself as precious, unique, and wonderful, what would you include in the description? Can you see the "self" that is unscathed by the hurt, the fears, and the doubts bestowed on you since birth? Can you see yourself like the newborn colt?

I believe this preciousness is hiding in all of us. We can see this preciousness in others and in ourselves when we open ourselves to its hidden splendor. Would your sense of yourself change if you were to honor this purity in your essence, your heart? Think about the possibility of allowing your preciousness to show up in everyday routines, in your relationships, and in your own quiet moments. You will find that by entering this process and delving into the hidden mysteries within that your preciousness will show up. You can measure the amount of preciousness you are letting shine through in your life by how highly you respect yourself. Nurturing the preciousness within you is one of the main requirements for self-respect.

Many of us can clearly see this innate preciousness in things outside of ourselves. To discover just what preciousness is, take advantage of this objectively and spend time with a puppy, a child, or an elderly person you think is wise and wonderful; or watch a butterfly or a deer roaming in the forest. When you witness preciousness in other beings, you will begin to see it in yourself.

You can expand your self-respect and self-esteem by coming to the realization that you can *live* from the place of preciousness in your daily life. Sometimes a place or an event can open the door. For instance, one of my coaching clients went back to the mountains where he grew up and he would swear the mountains said, "Where have you been?" This was a precious moment for him. It reminded him of the love and preciousness that connected him with his wife and the work he loved. This event provided the opening through which he saw the beauty and wonder of his life.

It isn't the words "I do" that give magic or meaning to life. The magic is in the words "I am."

Lessons of Love

— Melody Beattie

Dance With Your Emotions

Accepting yourself completely means loving and embracing your emotions, which of course means being aware of what they are. Mass media constantly assaults us with their reports about this tragedy, that political scandal, and economic ups and downs. If that were not enough, we create emotional soap operas and some of us have become junkies for the feelings that these stories evoke.

Feelings—emotions—make us laugh or cry, feel embarrassed or surprised, or allow us to experience both anger and pleasure. Feelings can be enemies or friends, but we must be aware of them and understand what part they play in our overall well-being. So, do you value your emotions? Are you afraid of them and, therefore, ignore them or attempt to repress them? Or, do you act out because of certain emotions? Do you take your feelings out on others? When you are angry do you lash out at others; if you are feeling sorry for yourself, do you try to make those around you feel sorry for you too? Or, do you incorporate your feelings into what you think, say, and do?

Feelings are never wrong. What they do is provide important information on the status of our spirit. It is possible, however, to mistakenly act out our feelings in a manipulative or hateful way, and in this case, although the behavior is wrong, the initial feeling is not. I contend that feelings operate like a message center, informing us about what is happening on the inside as a result of external experiences. We were never meant to judge our feelings as good or bad; all emotions are good because they are information and they are never wrong. They just are.

Whether we are aware of them or not, emotional responses determine most of what we do. At times our emotional response may be inappropriate. For example, we might accept a job or work for a promotion because we are afraid of financial insecurity. We might give a friend the silent treatment because we are angry. On the other hand, when we experience healthy love and have made friends with our feelings, we do thoughtful, appropriate things.

Can you talk about your feelings? Sometimes we think we are talking about our feelings when we're really talking about what we think. The opposite is also true. This confusion is likely to occur when we attempt to suppress our feelings or detach ourselves from them.

Unexpressed hurt can turn a person into a blamer or a victim, among other unhealthy stances. As I always tell my coaching clients: "Feel it now or have it show up unexpectedly later." Suppressed feelings can show up as depression, a habit of blaming others for unfortunate events, anxiety, or having a short fuse. Our emotional life is an intimate part of our well-being, for better or for worse. For this reason developing awareness about what you feel and expressing emotions promote balance and growth. Knowing what you feel while you are experiencing it improves overall self-awareness.

Unacknowledged emotions can show up at the most inopportune times. Repressing emotions—and thoughts, too—goes against our nature, the way we were designed. It is a little like refusing to acknowledge information about yourself and events in your life. So, if you refuse to experience your feelings you may turn your emotional life on its head; you may hold grudges, blame others, and become defensive. Continue down this unhealthy road and you may create emotional and physical difficulties. Experiencing emotions is key to a full life; repressing them is like using only half of yourself. Suppressing emotions also closes you off from receiving love and guidance, as well as giving it. Have confidence in your emotional life and let it be your friend, teacher and guide.

Behavior Patterns

You know the saying, "What you see is what you get." Your behavior patterns are what people see and these patterns have a big role in the quality of your life. They are both a cause and an effect, if you will, and manifest in your level of self-respect, the way you treat others and yourself. Your behavior patterns also manifest in the way you allow others to treat you. I believe that what—and who—you attract into your life is determined by the way you "show up." You either show your genuine, authentic self to the world or you show up with low self-esteem and lack of self-respect.

I have counseled many battered women. Although the particulars of their stories differ, these women shared the common trait of self-defeating behavior patterns. They made choices that kept them vulnerable and in danger. Their verbal and nonverbal behavior sent messages that determined how they were treated.

When I was in high school my mother taught me how to sew and I began to make my school clothes. Other girls often admired my outfits. In response to their comments, often I would say something like, "Well I made it," or "I didn't sew the sleeves in just right," or "Gosh, I should have gathered the waist in a little bit more." Before long, these same girls responded in kind with things like, "Oh, let's see what rags you have on today." Sometimes my friends would say, "I love your outfit," and then immediately begin to mimic the way I cut myself down.

My behavior represented an interesting mirror in that it showed lack of self-respect so disrespect is what I attracted. Ironically, even though I was on the homecoming court and considered to be "cool," my classmates made fun of the clothes I made because I had, without realizing it, invited that behavior. Soon, I developed a physical response to kids poking fun at me and my home-made clothes and I began feeling sick to my stomach early in the morning before I left for school. Looking back, I can see that my stomach hurt because of the pain in my heart. I craved acceptance of my sewing abilities, especially in high school, and I wanted to enjoy wearing my own creations. Sadly, my disrespectful behavior towards myself about my talent and creativity brought similar disrespect from others. Can you identify areas in your life in which your disrespect of yourself is sabotaging a positive outcome?

When I started saying a simple thank you and mentioning that I liked a particular pattern or fabric or asking for feedback about the color I chose, the comments became positive again. True self-respect means that your behaviors match your words. To achieve this, focus on being peaceful within and behave accordingly. This brings congruence in thoughts, emotions, and both verbal and nonverbal behavior. Remember a fundamental guideline: behaviors that send positive energy beget positive results; negative behaviors attract negative results.

Intellectual Awareness

To examine your thoughts and beliefs consider the following questions:

• Do you wonder if your life would be different if you didn't have negative self-talk chasing you around, punishing and judging you?

• Are your beliefs or thoughts infused with purpose?

• Are your thoughts focused and clear?

• Do your beliefs support a life theme, or are they whimsical and ever changing?

• Are your thoughts about yourself and your life critical and punitive?

• Do you approach your life with negative or positive beliefs and thoughts? Do you believe George Bernard Shaw's statement:

"Our lives are shaped not as much by our experience as by our expectation."

• Are you aware of your expectations in life? Are they congruent with the way you manage your daily life?

If you use self-awareness as a tool that enables you to explore your thoughts then you are free to mold them to match who you really are and reflect what you want from yourself, your relationships, and from your life in general. I once had a client who'd had just about every plastic surgery procedure imaginable. She also had an overwhelming need to be in a loving relationship. When I asked her to tell me the strongest, negative belief about her relationships she said, "I'll never be good enough." I asked her if she would be willing to give up thinking of herself that way. She said yes, but it was not as easy as simply saying the words.

As we worked on this issue, she realized how much she had incorporated her belief that she wasn't good enough into every area of her life, including relationships. I asked her to reverse this belief for one week by thinking in the opposite extreme and behaving as if the new belief of being good enough were true. Thinking about herself as good enough made her realize how much energy it took to maintain a poor self-concept. The negative belief left her preoccupied and she suffered from expending so much energy to keep the false belief alive. I told her that when all her energy was not tied up in negative thinking about herself, she might have some left over to put into a relationship, and as it turned out, she did. My client's experience demonstrates that your belief system strongly shapes life decisions, relationships, and well being.

Summary

Our dreams come true when we are true to ourselves. Self-love and self-respect set in motion your personal "spirit dances" and attainment of life's truest, most sincere longings. Authenticity holds the key to the future you desire.

Spirit knows who you are and is at your beck and call. He knows your inner strength and invites you to step inside the deepest dance your heart can bear.

— MELANEY SREENAN, PH.D.

Meditation/CD

Go to your quiet space. Begin to slow down...shift into low gear. Begin breathing slowly. Connect your breath with your abdomen, feeling it rise and fall as you breathe in full, deep, long, generous breaths, and then breathe out slow, long, breaths through your nose. Take five more breaths. Five, going deeper. Four, slowing down and connecting with your breath more and more. Three, shifting gears down, down. Two, slower and slower, feeling all the tension and stress falling away. One, down, down, more and more. Breathe into that place that takes you deeper and deeper. Settling into that place you find peaceful and wonderfully warm and inviting, finding within you the warm and safe place where you feel comfort and peace. Going down deeper and deeper...slowing down more and more.

When you are ready, and feel calm, quiet, and peaceful, connect with your negative voice. Stop now and tiptoe softly in the back door to visit your inner critic. Listen to the noise and chatter. Allow yourself to step fully into the self-critic mode and listen. Listen to the judge repeating over and over the words from which you busily try to distract...perhaps using the radio, food, TV, and a hectic lifestyle. What is the intention of this inner critic's voice? What are the words it uses to describe you? Are these words familiar? What is the inner critic saying? Whose voice does it remind you of? It could be a friend, a sibling, a teacher, a parent. When you are ready, ask this judging critic to sit beside you. Invite him or her to tell you its biggest motivation for saying all these negative things. What does it want from you? When the inner judge is finished explaining things to you, thank him or her and make a note in your mind to remember what this part of you is trying to accomplish. Perhaps your inner critic is trying to keep you safe or drive you or keep you from taking on too much.

When you are ready, check in with your genuine self. Ask your genuine self to give you advice on how to work in a positive way with the energies that drain you and let you sink into self-doubt. Ask yourself about the state of your dreams. Almost there? Or are you staying too busy to address them? Are your dreams and your life immersed in self-doubt and defeat or excuses? What things from *childhood immobilize you as you seek your genuine self? What message does your inner child have about what it needs to feel self respect? What does it need from you this week? How do the inner critic and the genuine self influence who you are, and what you really want?*

When you are ready, thank your inner wisdom for this conversation and slowly, gently come back to your safe place. While still in this meditative state, write down the insights you have received from this meditation. Write the answers to the questions in the meditation.

Fieldplay

Answer these questions in your journal:

1. Write the answers to the questions in the meditation, if you have not yet done so.

2. Describe in living detail your true genuine self.

3. Describe what disrespectful tapes you knowingly play in your mind. Next, write respectful words to counter the disrespectful ones. Then, write the positive words on Post-It Notes and place them someplace where you will see them daily.

4. How is your self-esteem? List at least ten strengths and ten achievements. List ten limitations and ten disappointments. Focus on and keep adding daily to the list of achievements and strengths.

5. Write a love letter to yourself describing your preciousness. If you can't write from the first person then think of a person who loves and adores you and write it from their perspective.

6. List five things that really hold a negative emotional charge for you. They can be found in the grudges you hold or the defenses you have. Take on, let go of, or resolve each one this week.

7. Ask five friends what you most commonly resent and blame. Ask the same five friends what they most like about you.

8. Write down the feelings that present the most difficulty, and then take the one emotion that stands out above all others and discuss it with a trusted loved one or friend. Come up with five ways to express the emotion in a healthy way. You will know the mode of expression is healthy because it will feel right to you.

Daily Play

1. Have a positive self-esteem day. You will engage only in positive self-talk and each time you catch yourself with a negative thought about yourself, acknowledge it and replace it with three positives. Create numerous ways to correct your behaviors. For example, each time you notice critical self-talk, immediately say the three positives out loud.

2. Be an advocate for yourself. Watch for instances in which you mistreat yourself or allow others to mistreat you.

3. Check your self-respect and see the way in which it manifests in your life. List self-talk statements that have come from former teachers or other authority figures. Then create positive statements to cancel each negative remark on your list. Repeat the positive sayings to yourself once a day

4. Make a list of your top five, strongest thoughts and beliefs, those that run your life. Then modify or disregard any thoughts and beliefs that serve only to limit you. Even if you only try it for one day, it is a powerful exercise and can change a lot of things in just that short period of time.

5. Next, take the most limiting thought or belief you have and write it down; then list all the things that justify it. Feel how attached you are to it. Next, trade it in for a different belief, a positive one. Write the new, positive belief down. Be ready to watch it change your life for good.

Resources

Succulent Wild Woman: Dancing with your Wonder Full Self, Sark; Fireside Books, 1997.

Claiming the deep knowledge of yourself and living life to the fullest.

Take Time for Your Life, Cheryl Richardson; Broadway Books, 1998.

Easy to use guide that challenges the readers to live their best selves. Shows you how to create the life you love.

Self-Care Cards, Cheryl Richardson; Hay House, 2001.

Self-Care Cards are a deck of fifty-two practical and inspiring cards that will show you how to take care of yourself. These cards are designed to support you in changing your life one week at a time.

The Psychology of Self-Esteem, Nathaniel Branden; Bantam Books, 1983.

Great guide to improving Your Self-esteem.

Something More. Excavating your Authentic self, Sarah Ban Breathnach; Warner Books, 1998.

This book challenges you to uncover your buried self and to attend to your longings and unfulfilled desires.

CHAPTER 5

CREATE HEALTH
AND WELL-BEING

Spirit taught me to race with the wind once in a while.

— MELANEY SREENAN, PH.D.

An integral being knows without going, sees without looking,
and accomplishes without doing.

— LAO TZU

believe that the best way to health is through the heart. A healthy heart is necessary not only for good physical health, but for emotional connections as well. Scientists and researchers such as Candace Pert, Bernie Siegel, and Rollin McCraty posit that, in one way or another, the heart has a mind of its own and can act independently from the brain. McCraty is a California scientist who helps individuals train their hearts to beat at a healthier level. He teaches methods that involve thinking more loving thoughts and thus his clients encourage their hearts to beat with a more "loving rhythm."

McCraty's research demonstrates the way in which emotions change the electrical charges within our bodies and consequently affect our heartbeats. Using an electrocardiograph machine, research subjects were asked to recall something that made them angry, and with that thought, their heartbeats became ragged on the screen. According to McCraty's research, if a pattern of angry thoughts becomes an individual's habitual day after day way of responding, this causes both emotional and physical imbalances. The physical imbalances often include dramatic fluctuations in the levels of the hormones DHEA and cortisol.

Anger and fear can cause dramatic shifts in the stress hormones and increased heart rate is associated with stress. The stress response is normal when we confront dangerous situations or have a temporary anger response. Our bodies are equipped to release stress hormones to help us deal with emergencies—these hormones can save our lives and trigger the "fight or flight" response. However, too many people stay in a state of emotional and, therefore, hormonal "emergency." Most researchers agree that constant surges of these adrenal hormones may age us, promote cardiovascular disease, reduce our immune function, and adversely affect our memory.

McCraty also asked research subjects to think about something loving, which again dramatically changed their heartbeats. As the September/October 1997 issue of *Natural Health* magazine reported, "This smoother heart pattern—a 'love signal'—is associated with numerous biochemical, hormonal, and nervous system changes in the body." In short, McCarty's Heartmath Institute teaches people how to alter their heartbeat to "produce health, joy, and love."

Journalist Bill Thompson reported in the same article that after spending the day at the Heartmath Institute learning a smoother heart pattern, he found the research to benefit him both physically and emotionally. The following quote from Thompson's article clarifies this phenomenon: "Scientists agree that since the heart generates the body's most powerful electric field, it pulls or entrains other energy fields into alignment with it, including the brain's. When this happens, the two branches of the nervous system come into harmony, and the brain becomes more alert, feelings of anxiety are reduced, and many favorable hormonal and immune system changes occur."

The folk wisdom of heart's desire and gut feelings has been scientifically confirmed....The heart not only has its own intelligence, but its own nervous system which acts as a radio broadcast system which is influenced by our perceptions and beliefs.

Q-Metrics

— CANDACE PERT, PH.D.

I have heard about individuals who make a connection between emotional and physical trauma and I believe this connection is real and deserves attention. For example, I have spent many hours with cardiac, cancer, and AIDS patients. Many of these men and women sensed that a preceding emotional event was linked to their current physical problem. One heart patient told me that her heart had hurt ever since her son died in a car accident. An ovarian cancer patient said that her husband's affair was eating her alive. Another heart patient told me her heart was breaking because her daughter was leaving the country to do undercover work. An AIDS patient said he had lost the best job opportunity ever offered to him, that it was killing him, and he didn't have the energy to go on. A bone cancer patient lamented that her children had all rejected her and it hurt her to the bone.

How we think often determines how we feel and influences the way we heal from serious illnesses. In his book *Love, Medicine and Miracles,* Dr. Bernie Siegel discusses the role of maintaining a positive attitude even when enduring a life-threatening illness. After many years spent treating individuals with cancer, he came to believe that a positive outlook may dramatically affect the outcome. Positive thought processes, including a strong belief in one's own power to heal, have been known to increase the chances of overcoming a disease. Endless examples exist of people with serious, terminal conditions who have experienced a positive outcome at least in part because of the way they coped and the attitude they adopted about the condition.

When I was a graduate student working in a hospital, I observed that most of the energy around me was used to label patients based on disease. A person became "a cancer" or "the appendectomy in Room 14." But the patients themselves had to rise above the labels in order to heal, and eventually I was inspired to teach a course on the emotional aspects of illness. I wanted to investigate the connection between emotional trauma and subsequent illnesses. In talking with many patients, I found a strong connection between the mind's thoughts or the spirit's desires and their physical condition. More than anything, these patients confirmed the idea that we can't separate the mind, the body, and the spirit.

I am *not* saying that people create cancer and that if they have a disease it is their fault or their doing. However, questions in medical science about why we have disease and why some people live while others suffer or lose their lives remain unanswered. While we have much to learn about the way attitudes and emotions may precipitate disease, we do know that a powerful connection between the body, mind and spirit exists within us that may be able to give us the answers we need to heal. For example, early studies about human connection reported that infants who were not touched did not develop or thrive normally and died. In the May 1986, results of a study at the University of Miami Medical School reported the advantages of "tactile/kinesthetic stimulation on preterm neonates." In this study, half the premature babies, the control group, were given intensive medical care but they were not touched in ways other than what was required to care for them. The other infants in the study received the same intensive care but also received tactile/kinesthetic stimulation, which involved three fifteen minute sessions per day of someone reaching into the portholes of the cribs and wiggling them or stroking them. They found that even though all the babies were fed the same formula on demand, the babies touched frequently gained forty-seven percent more weight than the control group over the same period of time. The touched babies were not only more active and alert, they also were able to leave the hospital a week earlier than expected.

It is clear that emotions play an integral role in our health and well-being. You can talk to two cancer patients with the same diagnosis and prognosis and the one with the optimistic, positive outlook will probably live longer with a higher quality of life than the one with a pessimistic, negative attitude. The point is our bodies and our minds are intimate friends and partners in everything we do and think.

It doesn't matter what you think because without emotion it would have no meaning to you.

Q-Metrics

— CANDACE PERT, PH.D.

Prayer has a Role, Too

In recent years some interesting studies show that healing among hospital patients as much as doubles when they are prayed for, even when those who prayed didn't know the individuals for whom they said prayers. The September 2002 issue of *O Magazine* reported on a study performed by psychiatrist Elisabeth Targ. She enrolled 20 patients with AIDS and then randomly assigned them to two groups. One group received prayers from experienced healers and the other group did not. In this study, the patients and healers did not meet and the patients and their doctors did not know when they were being prayed for. The results were dramatic and even surprised Dr. Targ. A full 40 percent of the control group died, but no one in the group being prayed for died during the six-month trial period. This study, and others like it, are a testament not only to the power of thoughts and prayers to affect ourselves and others, but also remind us that we have only begun to tap into the positive uses of this energy.

Diet and Well-being

How would you describe your diet? Do you consume whole, organic, living foods? That seems like an obvious question, but few of us think about the consequences of hurriedly eating while making tough decisions and concentrating on anything but the food we are hastily swallowing whole. Do you eat at your desk or standing in the break room? At night do you consume your meal standing in front of the refrigerator? Do you throw something in the microwave and devour it while talking on the phone or watching TV? If you are doing any of these things, they are most likely affecting your overall well-being. Not honoring yourself enough to make time for the food you are eating can cause heartburn, obesity, and poor digestion and assimilation of food.

A larger question concerns conscious eating—actually paying attention to the taste and texture of each food you consume. Health professionals recommend conscious eating because it promotes stronger digestion, which boils down to cleaner burning, assimilation, and elimination. Think of mealtime as a chance to slow down and connect with yourself, to send some love and nurturing your way, and to refresh and revitalize your body, mind, and spirit. Some of the most significant diseases start with poor diet and faulty digestion. Overall, neglecting the body's nutritional needs creates a great deal of stress.

I think the core of your well-being rests with your physical health. Dr. John Douillard, a mentor of mine on health and fitness, wrote *The Three Season Diet*, in which he emphasizes the importance of eating in a positive setting and also giving your body some relaxation and even a slow ten-minute walk after your meal. He recommends eating your biggest meal between noon and two because that is the best time in the body's daily cycle to digest and assimilate nutrients. His book provides examples of the well-being his patients have attained by following this seemingly simple advice.

Dr. Douillard also speaks about the value of eating seasonally, meaning choosing foods as they occur in nature, which means they are fresh. He contends that eating foods in their freshest state is the best way to attain and maintain your highest state of health. So, eating healthful, attractive meals in a relaxed, peaceful environment with a calm and clear mind is the optimal setting for you to receive full benefit from your food.

Several ashrams in the U.S. and elsewhere require complete silence at meals. Give it a try and see how you feel. Individuals practicing silence during meals report an absence of indigestion, heartburn, and bloating, and less fatigue after the meal is over. They also report eating less but feeling more satisfied because they were conscious of the food they consumed. Contrast that with the rushed "shoveling" of food so common at mealtime in our hectic culture. For many of us, the concept of conscious eating is brand new.

Although it's difficult to believe, many of us forget that food is meant to be nourishing. Ideally you should nurture your body with unprocessed, natural food that retains its nutrients. Considerable research confirms the adage that "we are what we eat." Stories abound of people who cure life-threatening illnesses or major health problems with a diet of natural, often organic, fresh foods. Eating nutritious food can make the difference between feeling your optimal best and dragging through your day complaining about being tired. For overall mental, physical, and spiritual well-being, make your diet a priority.

Your attitude about the foods you eat influences the way your body receives, processes, and metabolizes your meal. What you do and how you feel while you eat also determine how your body absorbs the ingredients you offer it. Eating should involve the senses and this is possible when you eat consciously. Do you know how your food tastes? What aromas does your meal offer? Do you properly chew and savor your food before swallowing it? What does it feel like in your mouth? Does your body like your food choices?

From time to time I teach a course called "Slim Healthy Lifestyle." One of the exercises involves having participants bring three portions of their favorite comfort food to class. As you know, we all have comfort food we long for when we are stressed or upset. For example, the oatmeal cookie that grandma used to make calls to us when we feel tired or overwhelmed. As the first step, I ask them to put the food in their mouth and hold it, no chewing or swallowing allowed. I then instruct them to close their eyes and just notice what it feels like in their mouth. Many people report that they taste an oiliness or bitterness or feel a texture that is not pleasing. For the second step, I ask them to put the food in their mouth again and chew it for one minute. Needless to say it becomes very mushy in the mouth and liquefies. By the time a minute is up many people are spitting the food out and saying that it tastes awful. In the third step, I ask them to put the last portion of food in their mouth, to let it sit in their mouth for thirty seconds, then to chew it for thirty seconds and, finally, swallow it.

This exercise is all about staying in the moment with a favorite food. It is common for participants to be turned off by the taste and texture of the food they once loved and craved. They become aware that a food they thought they loved really was a comfort food for their mind and not something that made their body feel good after all.

The Top 10 Reasons Diets Don't Work

After working with men and women who struggle with their weight, which often fluctuates up and down year after year, I have come to understand why diets do not work. Every year, people who want to lose weight spend over 40 billion dollars on books, tapes, special foods, programs, diets, various pills, herbal preparations, shakes and who-knows-what-else. Unfortunately, less than five percent of those who lose weight actually keep it off for more than one year.

It's easier to cure cancer than it is to lose weight and keep it off for two years.

Diets Don't Work

— GISELLE ANDERSON

Some of the reasons diets don't work are as follows:

1. **They are short-term.** Yes, they help you lose weight, but they don't offer long-term results.

2. **They are restrictive.** By their very nature, they restrict the "dieter" from eating at certain times, or eating certain foods, which results in a sense (real or imagined) of deprivation.

3. **They can be forms of self-punishment,** i.e., "I was really 'bad' on my vacation. Now I need to go on a diet." Or "I ate my way through the holidays; I'm going on a diet on January 2nd." Diets begin to seem like a good way to "get a grip" and "get back in control." Unfortunately, while a diet creates an initial sense of control, it usually results in calamity when it collides with the reality of everyday life, the business lunch, the office party, family dinners, and so forth.

4. **They aren't practical.** Very often, a diet will require a variety of behaviors that are difficult to sustain in public, while traveling, vacationing, or just living "normally." For example, "Just drink this shake every day for breakfast, lunch and dinner," assumes you eat at home and never venture out.

5. **They aren't flexible.** Everyone has an "unusual" day now and then. Maybe it's the boss's birthday, or your in-laws' 25th anniversary party, or just a dinner out with your family. Quite often, diets don't allow for that and hence, make the dieter feel "bad" for participating in the everyday activities of life.

6. **They create deprivation.** It doesn't take long for the dieters to lose touch with their own hunger level and begin to focus solely on when they will next be able to eat.

7. **They do not lead to good eating habits.** Typically, a person will reject 70-80 percent of the eating prescribed by a typical diet as an act of independence from the diet. Rather than creating lifetime healthy habits, the diet creates polarization in eating habits.

8. **They lead to "Good Food" and "Bad Food" thinking.** Quite often dieters will feel good about themselves when they are eating the food on the program, but they feel terrible when they eat food "off" the program. The "good me" and "bad me" perspective, based solely on eating, begins to develop.

9. **The more we diet, the fatter we get.** Statistics show us that the more people diet, the more they usually gain during the following period of regression or rebound eating. Ask any "professional" dieter and you will hear tales of the yo-yo effect.

10. **Diets *are* not the solution, they *are* the problem.** People often develop eating problems or disorders because of dieting. The fastest way to create emotional eaters is to restrict their ability to eat normally.

Physical Activity, Health and Stress

According to research conducted by Dr. Janet Zand, and reported in *Energy Times* (November/December 2002), 80 percent of all major illnesses are stress related. These diseases include endocrine disease, cancer, infections and cardiovascular disorders. In a special health report from Harvard Medical School titled *Stress Control: Techniques for Preventing and Easing Stress*, Herbert Benson, M.D. states that "stress can negatively affect your health as well as your mood."

The U.S. Centers on Disease Control and Prevention (CDC) report that physical activity performed on most days of the week reduces the risk of developing or dying from some of the leading causes of illness and death in the United States. They have reported that regular physical activity improves health in the following ways:

- Promotes psychological well-being

- Reduces the risk of dying prematurely

- Reduces the risk of dying from heart disease

- Reduces the risk of developing diabetes

- Reduces the risk of developing high blood pressure

- Helps reduce blood pressure in people who already have high blood pressure

- Reduces the risk of developing colon cancer

- Reduces the risk of depression and anxiety

- Helps control weight

- Helps build and maintain bones, muscles and joints

The CDC also reports that millions of Americans suffer from illnesses that can be prevented or improved through regular physical activity. For example:

- 13.5 million people have coronary heart disease

- 15 million people suffer from a heart attack in a given year

- 8 million people have adult onset diabetes (non-insulin dependent diabetes)

- 95,000 people suffer from a hip fracture each year

- 50 million people have high blood pressure

- Over 60 million people, a third of the population, are overweight

- In the year 2000, the cost of obesity in the United States was more than $117 billion

- Poor nutrition and physical inactivity account for some 300,000 premature deaths in the United States each year

You can't pick up a paper or read a magazine that doesn't report the importance of exercise as a means of maintaining your health. The National Institute of Diabetes and Digestive and Kidney Diseases (NIDDK) provides the following information:

Between 1991 and 2000, the greatest increase in obesity was found in the following groups:

- 18 to 29 year olds,

- those with some college education,

- Hispanics, and

- those living in the South.

Groups of adults that have the highest rate of obesity:

The BMI, or Body Mass Index, is a term developed by the National Institute of Diabetes and Digestive and Kidney Diseases (NIDDK.) BMI is a direct calculation based on height and weight, and is not gender specific. It does not directly measure percent of body fat, but it provides a more accurate measure of overweight and obesity than relying on weight alone. BMI, as developed by NIDDK, is determined by dividing a person's weight in kilograms by height in meters squared. Using the definition of obesity as a BMI of 30 or greater:

- Women – 26 percent of all adult women are obese, while 20.6 percent of men are obese.

- Among women, obesity rates are higher among minority women – 39 percent of black women and 36.1 percent of Hispanic women are obese.

- Adults aged 55-64 years have the greatest percentage of obesity, for both men (29.2 percent) and women (33.7 percent).

Why so many people are overweight or obese

- Behavior – eating too many calories while not getting enough physical activity.

- Environment – home, work, school, or community can provide barriers to or opportunities for an active lifestyle.

- Genetics – heredity plays a large role in determining how susceptible people are to overweight and obesity. Genes also influence how the body burns calories for energy or stores fat.

- Behavior and environmental factors are the main contributors to overweight and obesity and provide the greatest opportunities for prevention and treatment.

Many American children are overweight

- Today there are nearly twice as many overweight children and almost three times as many overweight adolescents as there were in 1980.

- Results of the National Health and Nutrition Examination Survey (1999) showed that 13 percent of children and adolescents were overweight.

Many American adults are overweight

In 1999, an estimated 61 percent of U.S. adults were either overweight or obese, defined as having a body mass index (BMI) of 25 or more.

- In 2000, a total of 38.8 million American adults met the classification of obesity, defined as having a body mass index score of 30 or more.

The positive effects of exercise, including improved balance and overall well-being, have been confirmed over and over again. Obesity is epidemic and stress is our number one killer. Exercise has a positive effect on both obesity and stress. Many medical studies have linked stress to both heart disease and stroke (Harvard Medical School, Special Supplement, *Taking Control of Stress*.) It is now time to ask yourself what physical activity you are doing to relieve the stress in your life and to help your body operate at an optimal level. You cannot afford to ignore the statistics presented above.

When Fitness Becomes Routine

The International Health Research and Statistics Association (IHSA) reports that January is the month in which most people join health clubs. The skyrocketing gym memberships and increased sales in exercise gear go hand in hand with New Year's resolutions of losing weight, getting into shape and an attitude of "fresh starts." The IHSA also reports that although the population of frequent health club attendees has soared by 154% since 1987, up to 135 million in 2000, the average attendance was only 88.6 days per year. Usually within two months new gym or health club members no longer go, and all the associated gear has been relegated to the back of the closet or stashed in the basement. By March 1, the fierce determination to get on a treadmill at the gym has faded away to nothing.

The common thread of having an unrealistic expectation of what will actually work runs through failed fitness programs. Men and women blindly go to the gym and have a personal trainer weigh and measure them and tell them what to do. All the while the body and mind are screaming "No! No! Run!"

The whole person needs to be considered when planning a lifestyle of fitness and well-being. My dear friend Beverly had to be at work at 7 a.m. and had family activities to tend to after work. The best time for her to get her workout in was at 5:30 a.m. She liked getting up well before that and having a cup of coffee and reading her Bible before meeting me at the lake to run. Since we lived in the heat and humidity of Florida, it was more pleasant to run in the cool light of dawn rather than in the late afternoon heat. She found getting her exercise in first left her more relaxed as she performed her job; this approach also eliminated daily arguments with herself about whether or not she was going to make it to the gym after work. Beverly wisely took her whole being into consideration in designing her exercise plan.

I also love the mornings for getting my outdoor fix because I believe I draw energy from nature. Getting up and moving first thing in the morning makes my head clearer and I feel more prepared to coach my clients. At four or five in the morning, I feel like I have God and nature all to myself. It is also a time of day that my clients usually do not need me. I feel totally relaxed and able to attend to my own needs. Later when I begin my workday, I am ready for it and feel focused and creative. I'm also ready to sit still and be fully present for my clients.

For other people, early morning hours just don't work, so they get out after their day is complete and a workout relieves work stress. Sometimes an activity is more readily available in the late afternoon or evening. Swimming, racquetball, and tennis, as well as health club aerobics classes, are generally available late in the day. Others like to incorporate exercise in their regular routine. For example, my neighbor walks three miles to work and three miles home every other day. Once exercise becomes part of the daily or weekly lifestyle, you will notice that you feel better every day. It's a universal experience.

I recommend taking a full month to evaluate your feelings about fitness and movement. Think about what you actually enjoy before you make any financial or social commitments. Monitor your energy levels throughout the day to see when your motivation to exercise is highest. As you expand your decision to take steps towards well-being, consider your lifestyle, which includes your family commitments and daily and weekly work schedules, volunteer responsibilities, and so forth. The millions of men and women who exercise regularly have learned to adjust work-out schedules to accommodate kids' soccer practice, day care arrangements, class schedules, social plans, and so forth.

When you have figured out what exercise you like and when it is best for you to exercise, set up a plan to work within a support system if necessary. For example, find a friend who will walk or run with you or trek to the gym for exercise class or a stint in the pool or on the treadmill. Don't forget to set up internal rewards or gifts to yourself such as a walk in the park, a visit with a friend, or a ticket to the opera or a football game as you reach certain key success levels. Make your well-being goals specific and measurable.

Find Support for Fitness Goals

I believe in creating support systems around your goals and this support can come in many forms. I propose multiple layers:

Layer 1: *Be clear about the program you have committed to because this layer is your internal support and is dependent on understanding the purpose for your plan.* If you intend only to lose weight or to achieve a short-term goal, then your plan lacks depth and success is less likely. Internal support comes from knowing how you will look as you embark on this journey of health and wellness. Visualize what you will look and feel like, and imagine how you will be different. This includes visualizing how your relationships, career, and life choices either will change or remain the same as you move further down the road to new levels of wholeness and well-being. This layer also involves an awareness of what you have allowed to sabotage your efforts in the past. How will you prevent this from happening again?

Layer 2: *Your environment must support you.* What do you need to clear away or to add in areas where you spend the most time? For example, if you have let the TV foil your attempts to eat nutritious foods because the fast-food commercials are so seductive, consider changing to HBO or some other station where there are no commercials. Or perhaps try getting up and walking around during commercials—or mute the sound. If you find yourself munching on cookies and chips, throw them out and replace them with an army of nutritious substitutes you keep handy for those times you have the urge to nibble.

Layer 3: *Support comes from the schedule you set up, as well as the flexibility and commitment you get from others.* Look outside your home for support if you have a partner who may oppose or sabotage your efforts toward well-being. Have someone you can call when you feel weak. Look around and form relationships with people in your life who already walk the path you're just beginning to walk. They can serve as people you emulate, and friends and mentors can help keep you motivated and focused. You can learn from those who have gone before you. Go ahead and ask them what systems and schedules they use to stay on track; then incorporate what works for them into your system. Most important, surround yourself with friends and acquaintances who will support you on your journey to improve your health. I strongly suggest you put this support system in place before you embark on your program.

When in Doubt, Do Something

I have a rule that if I am too tired or too busy to do my morning routine I still must get out of bed and do something, and I have a bag of tricks I use to keep myself moving forward. For example, I go to the location where I usually begin my run or to do my workout, and then I do some stretching. Sometimes after stretching, I find the energy to do the whole run or workout.

Even if I really don't have time or energy for the run or workout, I still begin my day with a delicious stretch. If after stretching I find I am still too tired, I go home and go back to bed if I have time. I am able to do this without guilt because I have done *something* that promotes my well-being. The rule that I must get up and out is an example of a personal support system I have in place. It gives me freedom to make a choice about how I will enhance my well-being that day, yet it requires me to apply some discipline.

Beverly is my dearest running partner of all time. Over the 20 years we were running buddies, she could have written a book of excuses about why she could not run on any given day. But because we gave each other support, she managed to rise above her excuses. This is why I suggest having a plan in place to use when you are unwilling or unable to do the scheduled exercise.

Meditation and Stress Reduction

In meditation we become available to our internal selves and hear the requests of the body, mind, and spirit. Reading about meditation and deep relaxation is not the way to learn these techniques. Training with a teacher, taking a class, or working with a mentor are far better methods. Listening to meditation and relaxation tapes is an alternate way to start a practice. However, statistics have shown that those who receive formal meditation and relaxation training obtain better results and tend to incorporate the practice into their daily lives.

A five-year study of medical care utilization statistics of 2,000 people in the U.S. who regularly practiced the Transcendental Meditation program found that their overall rate of hospitalization was 56 percent lower than average. The group practicing the Transcendental Meditation technique also had fewer hospital admissions in all disease categories compared to the norm, including 87 percent less hospitalization for cardiovascular disease, 55 percent less for cancer, 87 percent less for diseases of the nervous system, and 75 percent less for nose, throat and lung problems.

Our bodies are not wired to manage the stress that we experience in the fast-paced, hectic lives we have set up for ourselves. If the stress response is set off appropriately, it is an effective mechanism to help us function optimally in our day-to-day activities. For example, it would be appropriate to set off the stress response prior to competition, a presentation in class, or exam preparation. If the stress response is set off inappropriately or too often, a negative, cumulative effect occurs. For example, if you are late day after day for appointments or work, or are constantly over-obligated with home and work schedules, this leads to ongoing stress. Research indicates that most health problems affecting our society today, either directly or indirectly, relate to stress and the inability to relax.

Examples of stress-related health problems include the following:

- Depression
- Coronary heart disease
- Peptic ulcer
- Asthma
- Diabetes
- Lower back pain
- Headaches
- High blood pressure
- Arthritis
- Spastic bowel
- Ulcerative colitis
- Gout
- Cancer

- Skin rashes

- Accidents

- Multiple sclerosis

- Mental health problems

- Family violence

- Child abuse

- Suicide

Relaxation as the Opposite of the Stress State

Relaxation involves developing a frame of mind that elicits a physiological state referred to as the *relaxation state*. According to researchers at the College of Health, Physical Education, Recreation, and Teacher Education at the University of Wisconsin-LaCrosse, when a person achieves this relaxation state, a variety of physiological changes occur, including:

- Increased parasympathetic nervous system activity (the energy conservation branch of the nervous system)

- Decreased sympathetic nervous system activity (the energy expending branch of the nervous system)

- Decreased body metabolism

- Decreased heart rate

- Decreased blood pressure

- Decreased breathing rate

- Decreased oxygen consumption

- Decreased cardiac output

• Decreased muscular tension

• Increased blood clotting time

In addition to these physiological benefits of relaxation, there is scientific evidence that relaxation on a regular basis is beneficial to one's emotional outlook and other health areas. Researchers have found that relaxation, when practiced regularly,

• is enjoyable

• can decrease symptoms of illness such as headache, nausea, rash, diarrhea

• can increase levels of physical energy

• can increase concentration

• can increase the ability to handle problems and increase overall efficiency

• can increase social satisfaction (e.g., in dealing with family, friends, and colleagues) and feelings of self-confidence

• is helpful in the treatment of insomnia

• can reduce severity of spastic esophagus

• can reduce severity of colitis

• can improve airway resistance for bronchial asthma

• can reduce headaches

• can lower emotional arousal, which seems to explain why some individuals do not overreact to stress

In addition, researchers have found that people who report they relax on a regular basis:

• are more psychologically stable

- are less anxious

- feel in greater control of their lives than people who do not practice regular relaxation

- achieve a faster return to a balance or normal state after reacting to stress

- are more physiologically stable

Making it Happen

Like my friend Beverly, you probably have dozens of reasons not to exercise, meditate, and find ways to relax today. No doubt you've had times in your life when you made promises you were unable to keep—going to the gym every day and losing or gaining weight within a certain time period are just two examples. Perhaps you finished the preparation and have made the financial commitment and own the proper gear. Maybe you even started the program, but something was missing and like the average person, you quit in ten days to two weeks. You probably felt the inevitable let down, disappointment in yourself, and the guilt for spending the money but then having it all go to waste, along with the desire you started with.

One of the best ways to fail is to treat your current attempt to move toward greater well-being like past attempts. That is like stepping into old thinking, former patterns, and self-defeating behaviors, and it propels you in the direction of a negative, self-fulfilling prophecy. As a first step, focus on what is different about your commitment this time. Making it happen requires a unique approach and a promise to yourself to think only fresh, positive thoughts and to consciously look for new patterns to incorporate into your life. Refuse to link this attempt with any lurking in the past. Keep your energy, thoughts, and behaviors focused on the present—this is a different you, and this you is starting fresh.

The second step is to make sure you have set your plan up to flow with your life. No suffering, no martyrdom, no victims allowed! And the third step is to ease into this program with a sense of comfort, fun, and joy. It's essential to do the program without undo stress, which is why you should pick activities you enjoy. Drudgery, unrealistic goals, standards that are too high, and a desire to achieve ultimate buff by your second visit with a personal trainer will only set you up to be unsatisfied. Find ways for this program to complement your lifestyle rather than adding chaos and stress. Find a way for this program to flow down the river of your life with you, staying with you no matter what the river brings.

Physical Well-being

Since your body, mind, and spirit are connected, physical well-being cannot be separated from each other or from everyday life. It represents a dramatic part of the whole of life. So, how is your physical health? If your body were able to talk to me right now, what would it tell me? "Gosh, she loves me and puts healing thoughts and foods and activities into me," or "He keeps me hydrated and exercised." Or, perhaps your body might say, "I'm treated like he's trying to kill me—no exercise, never enough sleep, but then I am expected to go play serious basketball once in a blue moon with guys half my age."

Do you treat your body as if you value it, or do you operate with the idea that when you wear it out, you can just trade it in for a new model? Believe me, if we could get new bodies I would be the first one standing in line. But the truth is clear: If you wear this one out, you have no other place to turn. A nurturing physical attention means providing your body with the sleep, time, touch, nutrition, and the exercise it needs.

One of the first things I ask my new coaching clients is, "How do you feel about yourself?" The first area they address is the physical body and its lacks or needs. "Well, I'm tired all the time. I'm mega-stressed. I have 40 extra pounds I need to lose. I can't sleep." Without question, physical well-being is key to all the other things addressed in this book.

We often turn off the self-awareness dial on our physical self until we get sick. And then we are forced to pay attention. Are you guilty of that? Are you headed down the road toward illness? What about rest? Do you even know how much sleep your body needs?

What about how much touch your body needs? Are you meeting your needs to be hugged, held, and nurtured? Is your body's touch-indicator-light showing empty? Lack of touch will cause an infant to die, and studies have indicated a similar correlation among the elderly. With so many adults living alone and without family around them, touch deprivation is very common—and many people don't even think about the need for caring touch.

What about nutrition? Do you know what makes your body purr? Do you live on stress-induced adrenaline rushes and the energy roller coaster that goes with that? Do you know what individual nutrients your body needs? And, of course, we just discussed exercise. If you dislike working up a sweat and/or are too tired, stressed and always out of time when the subject of exercise comes up, address that issue now.

Summary

How effectively and joyfully we think, feel, and operate in this world has much to do with our physical well-being. Living life to the fullest and having the best there is comes from within. Dancing spirit must be fed and nurtured in all ways always.

Spirit speaks to joy, bliss and dancing wholeness as you reach oneness with your total beingness.

— MELANEY SREENAN, PH.D.

Meditation

Get into your quiet space and be sure that your spine is straight. You may either lie down or sit erect. Begin to connect with your breathing. Notice your heart and its pace. Breathe into this place and imagine sinking into warmer, softer, more settled space. Breathe in, and on this inhale imagine filling yourself with health and well-being. Breathe out, releasing any tension. Breathe in, filling your lungs and your abdomen completely. As you breathe this strong, powerful, full breath in, imagine it carrying you to new levels of health, wellness, energy, and vitality. Hold the breath for the count of three. Letting the air out, release old restrictions and old patterns. Breathing out bad habits and negative self talk...breathing in three full, deep, long breaths. Hold the last one to the count of three. One, sustaining you. Two, giving you energy. Three, bringing you complete understanding. Breathing out through your nose, releasing your breath into the space of quiet knowing. Feeling your inner energy join with your highest self in claiming your well-being. Slowly, gracefully creating a deeper connection with your body, mind and spirit.

Now imagine your body as a treasure chest. Go over to this treasure chest and pull out the things you love. Your big heart. That incredible mind. Those fit abs. Look around inside your treasure chest and see the good in you, the self-discipline and the constructive thinking. The brave and courageous you. Find in your treasure chest the things you love about your eating and exercise and being alive. Explore all the areas of this treasure chest, filled with your physical self and its well-being. Find the areas of most contentment and joy. Explore, discover, enjoy this process. Find more and more good and fun in who you are when it comes to well-being. Look for the balance you have created in your life and the good things you do to make your mind, body and spirit glow with health and wellness.

Now go to the bottom of this chest and find the things that served you in the past but no longer serve you today...things like pushing yourself until there is no more left in you...living at such a hectic pace you create more stress in your body than strength...or eating poorly on the run, as if your body didn't know the difference. Notice these things and take them out of the chest. Thank them for the service they provided for you at one time. Scan the chest for any thoughts, memories, or feelings that also no longer fit your wellness plan. Take all the now useless and disposable things, thoughts, and feelings and invite them to leave, evaporate, just disappear. Let go of any other things in your past that you need to let go. Scan your body, mind, and spirit for other indicators of stress, poor habits, destructive thinking, or bad memories and let them go as well.

Once you have cleared these things from your treasure chest, add anything you would like...perhaps eating only organic foods...cooking wholesome meals...feeling strong and energetic...regularly sleeping eight hours...having fun with your exercise routine...losing or gaining weight. Add whatever you need to your treasure chest. Keep adding things until you feel complete. Once you feel finished, step into a feeling of completeness and stay with it for several minutes. Acknowledge yourself for creating this great space. Embrace the wellness you feel inside this place. Step fully into the you that enjoys optimum health. Feel the energy and life vibrating within you. Thank yourself for this quiet time. When you are ready, come back to the room.

Now take your journal and write about all the things you liked that you encountered in the treasure chest. Once you have listed them, prioritize them from most important to least important. Write down the things that you most disliked in your process and list them in order of their destructive threat to your health and well-being.

Fieldplay

1. On a scale of one to ten, with ten being the highest, how stressed are you? Can you clear your mind, stop that racing? Do you use the idea of not having enough time to relentlessly motivate, push, and drive yourself? I invite you to sit down with a pen and paper and ask your body to tell you how it really feels about how you treat it and write a list

of what it says. Next, pick three items from your list and promise to change them for the better. In addition, take three things you are already doing to enhance your physical awareness and improve them by two points on that ten-point scale.

2. Keep a daily log of your current diet.

3. Try eating a meal in silence.

4. Make a list of the exercise you do.

5. What is your support system? Describe it.

6. How do you feel about yourself? Give an example and jot down what comes to you.

7. Take an inventory of your feelings and describe what you most enjoy. Include your energy levels in your inventory. When do you feel the most motivated to exercise?

Daily Play

1. Set up an exercise regimen that you can follow. The way to be sure to succeed is to be sure that your goals are specific, measurable and attainable.

2. As you create your plan, develop a support system and write it down.

Resources

You Can Heal Your Life, Louise L. Hay; Hay House Inc., 1999.

Hay's message is that if you will do the work, you can heal illness by addressing what you think and how you create your challenges.

Body, Mind and Sport: The Mind-Body Guide to Lifelong Fitness and Your Personal Best, John Douillard; Crown Trade Paperback, 1994.

This is my favorite book on complete understanding of your body type and exercise strategies for total body mind balance. Until recently, the effortless "Zone" of peak performance was only within the reach of serious athletes. Now, this book shows that anyone can reach the Zone, regardless of fitness level. Designed to accommodate a variety of individual fitness needs, the Body, Mind, and Sport program is split into two levels. Level 1 is for non-athletes who want to improve overall fitness; Level 2 is for those who want to train for competitive or recreational purposes.

The Three Season Diet: Solving the Mysteries of Food Cravings, Weight Loss and Exercise, Dr. John Douillard; Random House, 2000.

Solving the mysteries of food craving, weight loss, and exercise. This book makes sense out of all the diets and gives you clear and strong evidence for doing what your body needs for the ultimate in health and wellness.

Perfect Health: The Complete Mind/Body Guide, Deepak Chopra; Harmony Books, 1991.

This book focuses on discovering your body type and the way to eat to support your highest well-being.

Perfect Weight: The Complete Mind/Body Program for Achieving and Maintaining Your Ideal Weight, Deepak Chopra (Perfect Health Library); Harmony Books, 1994.

One of the two launch titles in the Perfect Health Library series by best-selling author Dr. Deepak Chopra, this book focuses on using Ayurveda, the ancient Indian science of life, to help readers conquer their weight problems.

Women's Bodies, Women's Wisdom: Creating Physical and Emotional Health and Healing, Christiane Northrup, M.D.; Harper. San Francisco, 1994.

A comprehensive book on women's health and healing.

Take Time for Yourself: Meditative Moments for Healthy Living, Ruth Fishel and Bonny Van De Kamp; Weston by Health Communications, Inc., 1995.

> These nurturing thoughts will inspire you to seek positive ways to grow each and every day of the year

Eating Well For Optimum Health: The Essential Guide to Food, Diet, and Nutrition, Andrew Weil, M.D.; Knopf, 2000.

> Dr. Weil provides readers with a program for improving lifelong health by making informed choices about food. He includes easy-to-prepare recipes in which the food is as sensually satisfying as it is beneficial.

Smart Fast Food Meals: How to Eat Healthy at the Top 12 Restaurants, Peggy Reinhardt; John Wiley & Sons, 2001.

> The author makes it easy to order lower-calorie, lower-fat meals by putting foods and exact fat, protein, carbohydrate content at your fingertips. It includes 48 different meals from the top 12 fast food chains—all totaling 700 calories or less, with less than 30 percent of calories from fat.

Eat Right 4 Your Type: Staying Healthy, Living Longer, Achieving Your Ideal Weight, Peter J. D'Adamo and Catherine Whitney; Putnam Publishing Group, 1999.

> The authors show which foods, spices, teas, and condiments help people of every specific blood type maintain optimal health and ideal weight.

Foods That Harm, Foods That Heal: An A- Z Guide to Safe and Healthy Eating, Reader's Digest Association, Inc.; Reader's Digest Adult, 1997.

> This is a guide to healing foods. It lists the benefits and disadvantages of foods and offers other nutritional advice on how to heal from disorders.

Eat Your Way to a Healthy Heart, Liz Applegate; Prentice Hall Press, 1999.

> The author shows you how her Simple Six Eating Plan can ward off cardiovascular disease naturally, helping you live a better, longer, more active life.

The Quest for Peace, Love, and a 24" Waist: Challenge Your Beliefs, Remember Your Spirit and Lose Weight With Joy, Deborah Low; Bonneville Books, 2001.

> The wise principles explored in this book will help you tune into the intelligence of your body.

American Obesity Association
www.obesity.org/welcomeAOA.htm
(800) 986-2373

> The AOA offers information on obesity, recent articles, membership information, a newsletter and a great little gadget to check your body mass index.

CHAPTER 6

CREATE POWERFUL RELATIONSHIPS

Spirit taught me each relationship is like the snowflake falling gently to the ground knowing no other just like it exists, and even so, at the same time, it is related to every other snowflake.

— MELANEY SREENAN, PH.D.

Love is like a mirror. When you love another you become his mirror and he becomes yours. And reflecting each other's love you see infinity.

Love

— LEO BUSCAGLIA

This chapter was both the most exciting and the most difficult to write. Relationships come in every size, color, shape, and dimension. Everything we encounter involves some type of relationship. Not only do we have relationships with parents, teachers, spiritual leaders, colleagues, children, adults, teens, and pets, but we also have relationships with inanimate objects such as cars, sometimes giving them special names, or with other objects that have special meaning to us. Many individuals have relationships with plants and gardens. The spectrum of relationships is so vast it can seem overwhelming.

I believe my next book will focus solely on the many types of relationships. Due to the complexity of the material involved in examining relationships, for now I have attempted to focus on romantic partnerships. Although the material deals with intimate, romantic relationships, it may be generalized and applied to other relationships you may have with children, co-workers, colleagues, friends, family and others. I briefly address some of these other relationships at the end of this chapter.

Everything we are and most of what we do involves relationships. The journey of love is one of continuous relationships, old and new, familiar and unfamiliar, and they always guarantee change. Each relationship is like the snowflake falling gently to the ground knowing no other just like it exists, and even so, at the same time, it is related to every other snowflake. Every snowflake is always different, yet always the same, which is the way we could describe relationships.

People are often unreasonable, irrational, and self-centered;

FORGIVE THEM ANYWAY.

If you are kind, people may accuse you of selfish, ulterior motives;

BE KIND ANYWAY.

If you are successful, you will win some unfaithful friends and some

genuine enemies;

SUCCEED ANYWAY

If you are honest and sincere, people may deceive you;

BE HONEST AND SINCERE ANYWAY.

What you spend years creating, others could destroy overnight;

CREATE ANYWAY.

If you find serenity and happiness, some may be jealous;

BE HAPPY ANYWAY.

The good you do today, will often be forgotten.

DO GOOD ANYWAY.

Give the best you have, and it may never be enough;

GIVE YOUR BEST ANYWAY.

In final analysis, it is between you and God;

IT WAS NEVER BETWEEN YOU AND THEM ANYWAY.

— MOTHER TERESA

I can trace my relationship journey back to my first love, my father. He was gentle, kind, and loving. He was always giving and there for me. When I was a baby, he rocked me to sleep at night with old Irish folk songs. Later on, as a successful young attorney, he would come home for lunch to give me horseback rides on his back as a way of trying to satisfy me until he could buy me a pony. Yes, I would say my journey with love began with my father. It seems clear that we are all meant to give and receive love; we are meant to feel love and be loved in return. During the early part of my journey, I was blessed with many individuals willing and able to take my hand and hold it when necessary. They stood by to see that I made it safely through the rough spots and at other times to guide me on my path.

As a teenager, I began to feel powerless. This stage started after a bout with encephalitis that left me with epilepsy and other health issues. Soon after, my parents began to talk about divorce. In order to control my feeling of powerlessness, I taught myself to ignore my emotions. I taught myself to put emotions in a file in the back of my mind in an attempt to have them leave me alone. I learned to be perpetually busy so that the overwhelming feelings wouldn't surface. It is clear to me now that I was afraid of my emotions because they made me feel vulnerable and transparent. To cope with this awkwardness with myself, I learned to focus on others and keep the attention off myself. I put on a happy face and detached from my authentic self.

Relationship Histories

Based on your childhood experiences, what promises or commitments did you make to yourself in an attempt to emotionally protect yourself in your relationships with people in general? These are the decisions we make based upon our observation of what brings acceptance and love from other people. Did you conclude: "No one really cares about me, so I will just stay cool and distant. That way, I won't get my feelings hurt." Did you learn how to be nurturing to others? For example, when your mate starts to tell you about a difficult and painful experience, how do you react? Do you finish his sentences, hush her, shut down, or one-up your partner by bringing up a worse experience of your own? If your mate exclaims how sore he is from playing ball and you follow with complaining about your own aching muscles from your long hike, you have just missed an opportunity to show love and compassion. Or perhaps you distract yourself by watching television or you change the subject because you lack interest or are unable to empathize. Do you find it hard to handle the emotional side of your relationships? Do you minimize your partner's views, reactions, or impressions by interrupting, saying things to make him or her wrong, or by telling him or her how to feel or what the *real* facts are?

We bring our ways of thinking, our habits, and our decisions from past relationships into how we operate in our current partnerships with each other. If we developed a collection of dysfunctional behaviors in our early interactions with people, it may be hard for us to change and create new behaviors. After many years of counseling and coaching, I've concluded it is inevitable that we attract people in our lives that will assist us in resolving the unfinished hurts, betrayals, and losses from former relationships and experiences of our formative years. It is common for adults to be stuck at age two or three when it comes to relationships and having their needs met. For example, if you were neglected, minimized, made fun of, or abandoned by one or both parents, your ability to give and receive love is stalled—your ability in this area is stunted. This is true even if the feelings of neglect or abandonment came because a parent was sick and in the hospital or suffered a major depression or other emotional illness. As an adult, you will most likely attract either a self-centered person, or a co-dependent person who parents and takes care of you. If one or both of your parents were alcoholics, you may choose someone who is addicted to alcohol, drugs, sex, work, or gambling.

Unfortunately, when it comes to emotional growth, we often pick up where we left off with our family. The developmental stage of two is concerned with having your needs met, and if you did not complete that stage or were violated as a youngster, you will most likely not know how to communicate your needs. As a result, you may find yourself unhappy in one relationship after another. It may have to do with not having your relationship needs met, or it may be that you don't even know what your relationship needs are. You may be unaware of your needs because in past interactions you have disowned these needs in order to be secure, accepted, or in control. What you bring to a relationship can be challenging, to say the least. Therefore, the more you know yourself and your needs, the better you will fare in the world of intimacy.

Many Levels of Love

There are many levels of love. The following section divides the different levels of love into categories. Your relationships may not fit perfectly into any one stage or level of love, and may be partly in one level and partly in another. The following definitions of the levels of love are meant to help you recognize at what level or levels you are functioning in your relationships.

- *Attraction,*

- *Consumption,*

- *Projection,*

- *The Renewal or Departure,*

- *The Commitment or Bond*

The Attraction: The attraction level occurs when we see one another and feel the physical, emotional, mental, and spiritual charge. This is the time of total excitement and we see only the best in this individual. We may play coy games and let our fantasies fly. Feelings of passion and warmth flow endlessly back and forth, reinforcing the love that is developing. The energy is strong, we exchange only positive thoughts, and we want more and more of one another.

During this stage, you probably feel lighthearted and carefree despite the world of reality trying to get your attention. The freedom you feel allows you to begin to share your deepest secrets and strongest dreams and desires. You think about the other constantly as you are trying the person on for size, so to speak. And all the while, you dare to fantasize about deepening the relationship with this new love. This stage usually lasts at least three months. It is a wonderful time because everything seems ideal.

Consumption: The next level is the consumption, and you take the initial excitement to the next level. You have explored the facets of your new love and it feels good. You like the fit, and you also experience feelings you haven't had before. Because of this, you want to put more time, energy, and attention into this love. Since the feeling is mutual, you are both on cloud nine, living in your own world. Sure you have met your soul mate, you may begin sharing dreams that may include marriage and family, depending on your stage in life.

In this stage, those around you notice the connection when they see you and your new love together or they hear you talk about the new person. Clearly, you are happy and focused on this new relationship, which often means your other priorities take a backseat. The relationship becomes *the* priority. And why not? Life is grand as this unspoken commitment unfolds. Very little conflict is involved at this stage, which usually occurs during months three through six.

The Projection Stage: The projection stage starts when some reality sets in. It involves coming down from cloud nine and those around you may be relieved when you are fully present and involved in your former routines. Rather than being in the midst of an all-consuming bond, you start spending time with your friends, turning your attention to work projects, and you show up at the gym again. This stage can be the last stage of the relationship if individuals reach this plateau separately. One may feel abandoned or lost by the seeming withdrawal of the other. Provided one or both possess some skills in conflict resolution, it is possible to get through this stage without ending the relationship. However, without some depth and a strong desire to go forward, this is often the beginning of the end. Lovers become a bit disillusioned when it becomes clear that life is not so perfect with this new love.

When trouble begins to brew, history rears its head and the dance of true intimacy begins. Individual wants, needs, desires, and fantasies are projected onto the other. They are often expressed indirectly and expectations surface, but they may remain unexpressed. When one person brings up these expectations it may be done with an edgy tone or with words that convey disappointment or anger. Quite naturally, this creates distance, confusion, and defensiveness.

Next come the power struggles, issues of control, and manipulation. This is the time the new partners question one another's love, or even their motivation for being together. The partners may engage in a dance of "come close, go away." Prior relationship and childhood histories play the biggest, strongest role here and many relationships fall apart at this point. For one reason or another, people decide they are not right for each other.

Interestingly enough, despite the disparity, sometimes people stay together out of need or insecurity and the truth gets shoved under the rug. In the best-case scenario, they learn to communicate, be authentic, and find a way to get their needs met and values honored. They do this while openly expressing expectations and desires, thus avoiding the manipulative dance, the "guess how I am feeling game," or the "look what you've done to me" blame game.

Some choose to stay together and play out the suffering, you-hurt-me-so-bad cycle again and again. Some engage in comparisons, such as "I wish you were like Maria's boyfriend" or "I wish you were more neat and thoughtful like me." This is a very challenging time for both parties if they choose to stay in the relationship.

The Renewal or Departure: This stage involves looking inward and being willing to honestly see the life you are creating around this relationship. This is usually a place where you review the last six to nine months to form a snapshot of what you have. Renewal is a calm, peaceful time, yet not without pain and confusion over what issues belong to you and what belongs to your partner. You question what needs to change, be fixed, and whether you can accommodate what is. Part of this process involves assessing the whole picture, together and apart, and summarizing who you are as an individual and as a couple.

This may be a place where one or both parties see the picture as dark and gloomy and make an exit. It may be a time when love is not enough to sustain the commitment the relationship requires. This can be a highly emotional phase because abandonment issues often take over and at times, this war with the heart seems desperate. If you stay together this is a deep, spiritual period and the union feels solid and laced with a more grounded love.

The Commitment or Bond: This can be the deepest and the most rewarding stage. The bliss of the new relationship comes into balance. For example, the roles and barriers, both internal and external, find a place in the way the relationship is defined. One or both parties may bring children and the demands of ex-partners into the mix. By this stage, it becomes clear that both individuals have separate lives and activities. This stage rewards couples for tenacity, and they experience a bond that is deep and settling because they share a deeper passion and their style of relating to each other has stabilized. All these elements are enhanced by knowledge of each other's needs and having built a foundation of unconditional positive regard. Deep, strong love presides over all and conflict and communication is constructive. Even in the worst moments both share a commitment to build the relationship and to resolve the upsets.

Letters

As we are flowing through the stages and levels of love, there is mind chatter and a body of thoughts and feelings that accompany our outer, physical experience. This inner experience is the very personal side of our thoughts and feelings and we may or may not discuss or share this with our partner. These expressions are full of our dreams and our expectations. They reflect our own unique experience of the current interaction and at the same time are colored and interwoven with the experiences of our past and our expectations for the future.

In the following letters, I have shared some of the inner thoughts and feelings that unfolded as my relationship with my former husband passed through the many levels of love. I thought these expressive letters would illustrate the flow of a relationship in a very special and personal way. It is my hope that these letters will illustrate the growth and maturity of thoughts and feelings as they might occur at each level in a love relationship.

LOVE LETTER FROM THE HEART:
THE ATTRACTION PHASE

Dearest Heartmate:

Loving you first from a distance. Teaching aerobics, you were always there. You made me smile. Jogs in the morning, chapel visits, long talks, lunches, evening trips to the yogurt shop, stopping in by work to leave a card...loving you from a distance.

From beneath the gentle touch of your heart...allowing us to move from a distance to the forefront...being without you became like living without air. We did everything together. We had the same values, work ethics, goals, hobbies, interests, and we had fun!

Touches, hugs, kisses, total harmony, loving unconditionally, shutting out the world – just you and me – carefree minutes turned into hours, no worries, no concerns, no bills or house, or yard chores. You always were as happy to see me as I was to see you.

You were on your best behavior then, every thoughtful thing I did for you meant so much to you. Our love was undefined and free of limitations or rules...loving you from beneath the gentle touch of your heart.

Loving you was without fear...without hesitation and without consideration of anything but a positive response from you.

As we got closer the excitement began to include fear...what does this mean...like a child playing in the park who turns to Mom and she's no longer there.

It All Starts With Communication

The three keys to communication are:

• Using the language of love and intention regardless of the conditions,

• Looking at and addressing the root issues,

• Committing to resolving the issues through listening with your whole mind, heart and soul,

• Let's look at each in detail.

Using the Language of Love and Intention:

Empathetic, loving, compassionate, and open communication nourishes the bond between two people and raises the bar on the level of the relationship because it conveys the message: "I care about you. You are important to me. I respect you. I honor who you are." Communicating can be successful and rewarding if you practice certain key principles. For example, the language of love and intention focuses on being fully present and clear that you want to experience and honor the love between you and watch it grow. It means that you choose love in your heart no matter how wronged or wounded you feel. To choose the intention of love means responding from a place that is calm, nonjudgmental, and loving. If you cannot do this, and you value your relationship, then don't communicate at all. If you are in the middle of an upset and are not able to maintain loving, calm communication, you must stop then and there, agree to take a break, and come back later to discuss the conflict.

The intention of love always needs to be the focus when you communicate with your partner. Intention has to do with the goal you create in your mind and heart about your desired outcome. Ideally, your intention is that after the communication about a specific issue is over, your relationship is more loving for having resolved the conflict—even if the resolution still eludes you.

Always ask if your loving intention is strong enough to survive ego and old thinking patterns. Will your intention to be positive conquer your need to be right, your desire to win? The strength of your positive, loving intention needs to be solid enough to overcome the mudslide of pain and disappointment lurking in your past. Your intention struggles to blend with any contentious flow in the conversation that is taking place in the present, not the past.

Love and intention, when joined together, ease the movement from hurt, anger, and fear to a place of safety and understanding. The language we use counts when we are holding on to intention. For example, "Help me understand what you are saying" or "What I heard you saying is that..." are non-defensive, non-sarcastic statements. And don't forget that your tone is as important as your words, as are eye contact and other body language.

This is the time to listen to the partner who is addressing a need or working to resolve a conflict. Listen with a full, open heart, and energy that conveys how deeply you care. Even when the receiving parties don't say a word, the senders should be able to feel the receivers wrap themselves around them in love and intention. Some ways that the receiving party can send positive regard to the sender is through open body language and eye contact. Open body language means uncrossed arms and legs and a still, relaxed demeanor that fully focuses on what is being said and communicated. The receiver should be looking into the eyes of the sender with full and nonjudgmental attention with an encouraging, open look on his or her face.

THE CONSUMPTION PHASE

Dear Courageous Spirit,

I remember when we got engaged and promised to be true to each other forever. It was a wonderfully typical evening of you picking me up at my house to get a frozen yogurt. You had managed to have my ring put in the yogurt, in a box of course. I remember I always thought the day you asked me to marry you I'd run away or just evaporate into fear. The night you asked to marry you instead of the reaction of fear I expected, I was so excited that I almost fainted with joy. I was so sure of us and so committed to you.

That same night I asked you to promise that you'd never change, and to my devastation and total shock you said "Melaney, the only thing that I can truly promise you is change...constant change." I felt like you'd just taken the ring back and stuck a knife in my heart all in one gesture.

Looking at and Addressing Root Issues

The second key principle is looking at and addressing the root cause of conflicts. I remember a newly married couple who came to see me. The wife was in tears. The husband seemed totally bewildered about what he had done and what to do to resolve the issue. She said that after three weeks of marriage he didn't love her anymore. He rose up and demanded that she *know* how wrong she was. He went on to point out all he did for her and what he'd always done for her. The more he talked, the more she sobbed. He finally sat down, shaking his head in disbelief. Then he looked at me and said, "How could she not know how much I love and adore her? Did you hear all the things I do for her?"

I gave him an empathetic nod, as she sobbed on. After a short pause, I asked her why she thought he didn't love her. She stopped sobbing and began to talk about how she loved riding bikes to the drive-in and having a picnic on Friday nights. That was how they met and it had been a ritual of theirs until three weeks before when he didn't want to go anymore. She felt the need to connect with him in the playful way they used to, but he said, "No, I don't care to." This new husband heard her request but did not hear the unexpressed need she had to relax and be playful and carefree with him as they had been before. She had turned his refusal to spend time together on a bike ride or a picnic into "he doesn't love me anymore," but never checked it out with him.

As for the husband, he completely missed the silent and deadly question, "Do you love me and want to play?" Instead of asking her the root cause of her pain, checking out what had her thinking that way, he instead jumped to his own defense, but with his heart still in a loving place and with the intention of resolving the conflict. He was missing the most important piece of information.

In actuality, both parties were in different places, thereby missing the point. She wasn't conveying her deep desire, and he wasn't addressing her emotions. When he saw that he was causing an unintended reaction in his wife, he needed to ask her something more. "What is that look of disappointment on your face? Did I just hurt your feelings?" At that point, it would have been her responsibility to tell him what she took from his words. He kept doing what he thought was best, which was pointing out how wrong she was. Not finding a way to identify the underlying emotions only makes the resolution of a conflict or upset more illusive.

Listening With Your Whole Mind, Heart, and Soul

The third principle involves being committed to resolving the conflict by listening with your whole mind, heart and soul. The couple in the last section fully intended to resolve their communication problem. They were not both jumping into the boxing ring with their boxing gloves on, ready to duke it out. This couple was boldly holding onto the goal of clarifying and resolving the dilemma.

One important rule in this principle is that you can't both be upset at the same time. The one who was upset first gets the floor until that issue is complete. So often one person will say something like, "I am so hurt you didn't greet me at the door after being gone five days. Didn't you miss me?" If the other person then gets defensive and says something like, "Well, I didn't know when you'd be home and you didn't seem like you were missing me much anyway," then this is an invitation for a heated and destructive encounter.

In a situation like this, it often takes considerable courage to respond a bit differently, "So you think I didn't miss you? I can see how you would feel that way because I was busy when you got home. Let me tell you how very much I missed you." Rather than responding in this thoughtful way, it is easier to give up, be distant, blame, engage in silent treatment, and justify your holding back affection and love. However, the easier path is contrary to fundamental principles of quality relationships and communication.

THE WEDDING:
THE CONSUMPTION PHASE - CONTINUED

Dearest Precious One,

I love you to the core. I promise to love, adore, honor and cherish you until death do us part.

You are my best friend, my confidante,

I promise to love you unconditionally and without judgment

To give you my all in all ways, always for the rest of my days

You are my love. You are my life.

Learning from the "First Love"

We learn about love from our first family. We shape our outlook based on how we were treated as we grew up, and by observing our parents and extended families' ways of being together. How did your parents express their love? Did they:

- say "I love you" out loud?

- touch, kiss, hug, and have a look of deep connection?

- argue and resolve disagreements in your presence?

- tease and play or hold grudges and pout?

- give each other the silent treatment?

- treat one another with respect and caring?

In other words, how did they show their love to each other? How did they love you? Did you get hugs and kisses and eye contact? Did you experience open communication and interest in how you were feeling or how things were going in your life? If you were sad, did they notice and did they show compassion over the reasons for your sadness? Did you feel validated by the way they looked at you, by the way they stopped what they were doing, moved closer to you, and gave you their full attention? Were you listened to? Did you get quality time? Did you feel cherished or like a bother? Were you valued and appreciated?

When you are loved unconditionally, you develop a healthy foundation you can count on as you grow up. How you feel about yourself and your level of self-love will determine a lot about how you approach relationships. I think that any relationship can succeed if you choose to trust, communicate openly, respect one another, and maintain clarity about your expectations and needs. Enhance your success by adding thoughtfulness, making one another a priority, and being willing to dance with each other's expectations and past wounds. Using the 50 percent rule, take responsibility for your own growth, and put yourself in the other person's shoes before judging.

In addition, learn to "fight fair." Fighting fair means that when you are upset you express how you are feeling without attacking, blaming or criticizing. It means hearing the other person's point of view, and being clear about what issue it is you want to resolve together and sticking to that issue. With these ingredients you can have a blissful relationship.

THE MIDDLE: THE PROJECTION PHASE

My Dearest Soul Mate,

It's New Year's Eve and what a year we have had. I want to wash away the betrayal, hurt and abandonment that has entered with deadly silence into our relationship. Your betrayal and my reaction..... .

I am emotionally, physically, spiritually and mentally starved for the man I loved so dearly in the beginning of our relationship. We have become like pen pals...notes read in the night. It is as if we've built this wonderful house piece by piece, a mansion, beautiful, rich, and radiant, and all of a sudden you don't live here anymore. You occasionally come to visit but for the most part I am left in the mansion alone to maintain something that I didn't even design. This place is something that I would have never built for myself.

I have tried to ignore the hurt and the pain. I have tried to work through it on my own. I have made excuses for you and blamed myself. I have tried to make myself look fresh and light and act vibrant after listening to stories of failing relationships and hurting souls all day long in my office, only to face the cries of the ghost of the mansion's dark side as I fling the door open at night and hear the whispers of a dying relationship, a breaking heart, filling me with my own emptiness, helplessness, and confusion.

How can I reach you? Will you visit? Will you stay? Are you coming home?

Helping a Relationship Evolve

Awareness that personal development is critical to both parties is necessary to an evolving relationship. It is helpful when both parties make a commitment to deepen the relationship by being willing to work on themselves, and to change and to grow with the changing needs of the relationship and their partner. Relationships tend to be enhanced wherein the partners have a great deal in common and do multiple activities together. These couples often report growing closer over the years. The natural human desires to be challenged, acknowledged, and stimulated are met in this type of relationship, and this strengthens the bond between the marital partners.

Creating a lasting relationship involves several steps and is an ongoing process. For example, we must all take responsibility for our own "stuff," be clear and reasonable in our actions, and stay true to ourselves and our own heart's desires. We also need to demonstrate appreciation to, gratitude for, and thoughtfulness toward the other person, as well as show willingness to compromise and offer compassion.

What or Who is the Priority?

I believe that people love to be loved, which leads to the need to feel as if they are the priority in a love relationship. Fulfilling the need for love is what most people strive for more than anything else in life; it truly is the most important body, mind, and spirit need. Treating your love relationship like it is the number one thing in your life is of prime importance to your partner's contentment and the longevity of the relationship. What thoughts or ideas come to your mind when you think about making your partner number one? In what ways are you already making your relationship your first priority? Remember in the beginning stages of the relationship when you could not even concentrate on anything other than your new love? All you could think about was when you would be together next. You spent most of your time thinking of things to do with the person and what talk about together. You wanted to please this new love. When was the last time you let the raw, ecstatic, "so glad to be in love with your mate" feelings fly?

When was the last time you tossed schedules and practicality to the wind, opened your heart, and connected with your loved one on a deep emotional level? How would that feel now? What is in the way of giving the relationship that energy you once freely invested? Putting your relationship first in the order of things is not always an effortless task; however, putting it first is a powerful tool that makes a statement about the quality of your commitment to your partner, thus reinforcing the depth of its importance in your life.

When couples come to my office for marriage counseling, one of the first things I ask them is if they can imagine themselves putting the relationship first. I ask them if they can agree to take twenty minutes every day to just be together, even if it is on the telephone during lunch break. If the answer to either question is no, I tell them I cannot help them. So, ask yourself the same key questions:

Do you have the desire or the will to put your partner at the top of your list?

Are you willing to take twenty minutes, any twenty minutes, and devote them to your partner?

Intimate relationships do not have to be hard, grueling work; however, relationships need *attention*. We live in hectic times and most of us talk (sometimes endlessly) about the demands on our time. We also live in times of constant change that challenge us to adapt. But the one thing we can keep solid is our partnership if we are willing to make it a priority, thus allowing our commitment to strengthen and grow.

RENEWAL OR DEPARTURE

Dearest Great One,

For now, it doesn't matter whether we agree or not, or who's right. What matters is what goes on between the two of us. You and me. Are we growing, changing, and loving each other? That is what matters to me.

Things around us, they're things, props, settings...the things we own, the places we go, the events in our lives... they are easy to chase after...and put first.

But the only thing that matters at the end of our stay on earth is how well we loved, the quality of our love...

As I face going to bed alone while you go to work, I hold you like never before with a depth and peace no love but mine can know. I remind you of the profiles of our love and courage and promise of foreverness. May I offer you with a world of stars, stripes, and banners in my eyes, a heart beaming with warmth and excitement for you, strong as a grown tree, energetic as a fresh Marine soldier, high as the hot air balloon, and as complete as the beauty of the full moon as it sparkles on the lake.

You are there and I am here and love is all that matters to me... I will wait in hopes that we cross this bridge together.

Taking Responsibility

Taking responsibility for your own "stuff" involves understanding the twist your past puts on your view of things, as well as keeping a check on the spin you bring to situations because of these experiences. For instance, if I believe you don't love me because I was led to question my mother's love, then I will have a tendency to put that idea out into the moment. So if my partner comes home late from work, forgets an anniversary, or overreacts to a disrespectful biting comment, then I may fall back into believing I am not lovable. So, taking responsibility means you must be willing to be wrong and vulnerable, and to examine automatic, hasty conclusions for their authenticity in the present moment and not as unconscious evaluations from the past.

Relationship Expectations

It is critical to stay in your heart and be clear about your expectations of any relationship. Your relationship will grow stronger when you let go of the part of you that wants to play it safe. What would it be like if you got rid of the tendency that chases you around and judges your every move, or screams, "Warning! Warning!" each time you open your heart? Staying with the voices in your head plays a major role in how your relationships evolve because that voice can be a self-fulfilling prophecy. Look at the ways your internal saboteur shapes your love relationships. When you think about emotions, love, and risk, what ideas fill your thoughts? Do you feel love or fear, hate or resentment? Black and white thinking can be dangerous, not only to the soul and your relationships, but also to your own individual, emotional growth.

By being clear about your expectations for your partner, you create greater intimacy because that sets the stage for your partner to feel safe about what you need and want. In addition, being clear means letting your partner know what really matters to you. It means communicating up front, leaving no room for second-guessing or misunderstanding. By making your expectations clear, specific, and measurable your partner will be open to you on the heart level and willing to be vulnerable in relation to you.

Being clear also allows for greater creativity and playfulness in the relationship.

For example, if I say, "Let's go off this weekend and relax," is this clear, measurable, and specific? What do you mean by "go off" or "relax?" More importantly, what is the underlying need in my request? Is it "Darling, I have been missing you and really want some quality time with you, to walk on the beach, to hold hands, to look into your eyes, and to tell you how much I love you? I want to go to the Heron House on Long Boat Key and watch the sunset and eat dinner at Bistro's. I want to walk and talk on the beach hand in hand. I want to sleep in with you in the morning and just wallow in your presence." See the difference? Your partner gets the deep intention you have to be with him or her. He sees how walking on the beach, talking, sleeping in, eating dinners out, and watching sunsets are part of your need to connect and be close.

The outcome of such a communication puts everyone on the same page. The nebulous "Let's go off this weekend!" reveals no meaning or intention. Even if I had said, "Let's go to the beach!" my statement still needs clarification and specificity. Otherwise you might assume I want to go to the beach to catch up on my work, sleep late, work on my tan, read a mindless book, or whatever. It's not that these activities cannot be enjoyable, but they may not meet my expectations for the weekend and lead to disappointment. In order for my expectations to be met, I have to let my partner know exactly what they are or the outcome of the weekend is left to chance.

Non-specific requests are a setup for disaster. When we do not clearly specify expectations, then our partners make assumptions. Disappointment and conflict can result unless you express the details about what really matters to you. When you are able to identify exactly and specifically what it is you are intending with a request and are able to state it in simple and straightforward language to your partner, it creates clarity of purpose. When both parties understand the intention of a request, it enhances the relationship satisfaction for both partners.

People say that relationships are work. I disagree. However, I do believe that like children, cars, or pets, they do need attention and time on a regular basis. Examine areas in your relationship that need your attention.

GIVING TIME FROM THE HEART: RENEWAL OR DEPARTURE

Dearest Spirited One,

I look at our lives and I feel so fortunate. I think of the love we have and the times we've had together. I feel so lucky, as if I've won the lottery.

As long as I stay in the moment I feel warm inside and blessed beyond belief. I feel light like a butterfly just out of the cocoon and free as a bird.

Forgive me, though, as I step outside the truth of any moment beyond right now and feel the cloud of doom and depression from the rigid schedules, endless work hours, and the passing in the night. A war rages inside my heart.

I long to hold the intimacy of our first years once again next to my heart. It seems these days we just keep promising to spend time together, as if promising were enough. I am fearful for the life of our marriage, as though it is being hunted down like an injured animal and soon, without mercy, it will be shot to death, unable to run anymore from the unattended wounds it has incurred along the way.

Time: A Gift of Love and Kindness

Time can be such a gift of love and kindness. So often I hear couples say that they feel like ships passing in the night. How can a relationship grow when individuals are apart? If no regular time is set apart to be together, what message is sent and received? Ask yourself the following questions:

- Do you want to send the message, "I don't have time for you?"

- Do you feel good about carving out time for your loved one?

- How do you feel about the time you do spend together?

- How can you enrich time spent together?

- Does time together just happen or do you plan for it?

We all have the same amount of time, 168 hours in a week. Calculate the hours you spend together as a couple. Being together at children's athletic events or social gatherings does not really count for the kind of time I am talking about. I am referring to quality time for the two of you. And when you are together are your needs and desires being met? Perhaps this area has been a rocky road. Perhaps you haven't felt good about deep, connecting time together because you are too tired and distracted. So often couples long to connect, to be together, and, when they do finally take a vacation once a year or plan an evening out, they end up talking about things that don't really matter. This continues the pattern of not connecting in ways that enrich the relationship. In many cases, both partners end up feeling empty and frustrated.

Taking time to talk about the intimate soul of the partnership strengthens the bond you have created together. Talking about kids, football, the weather, other people, the neighbors, events, or the budget and household chores hardly qualifies as intimacy. Intimate quality time together gets more and more difficult as times between encounters increases. This lack of attention to the relationship may lead to expectations being so high that disappointment is inevitable when the time to be together and to be intimate arrives.

Sometimes I am convinced that the most powerful and important gift partners can give each other is time. Give it fully and completely, and focus on the moment, the here and now. This involves taking a deep breath and reminding yourself about what really matters.

The type of connection I refer to here is free from the noise and distraction of all the "stuff" we have going on in our heads and all around us. This is why a child's sporting event or parents' night at the school may be enjoyable and valuable, but they are not occasions during which partners can focus on each other. Quality time for a couple allows the heart connection to come through, and we can think of it as easy, gentle, and loving. Being fully present means we have time to listen, to lend support, to be calm, and to create depth in our relationships. Time also allows us space to dream, laugh, cry, reminisce, listen to music, or tell stories. We need to renew and refresh, as well as regroup and redirect our focus and energy. In relationships, the most heart-felt satisfaction comes from giving time freely and regularly.

Sometimes spending time together in silence and looking deeply and fully into the eyes of your partner will connect your spirits without using words. It is said that the eyes are the windows of the soul. I believe that. Quietly observing your partner can enhance the bond of your relationship. When you are together, but silent, this allows a space for deep feelings to surface and be acknowledged.

Valuing Thoughtfulness

A healthy dose of thoughtfulness goes a long, long way because it sends a powerful message of "I love you and I care about you." Can you remember the last time you did something thoughtful for your partner? Do you get satisfaction out of being thoughtful? Thoughtfulness is a simple act from the heart that is intended to comfort, please, or help out, and most important, send your partner a loving message. Sometimes the most thoughtful thing you can do is to stop in midstream of activity or conversation and touch your partner. You might say, "Hey, I love you and I think you are so wonderful—or handsome, beautiful, incredible... ." You can find the right word.

When I was growing up, great value was placed on thoughtfulness in our home. Every week we had a family "pow wow." I call it a "pow wow" because there were six boys and three girls in the tribe, and we all were very close in age. During our weekly check-in with each other, we voted for the most thoughtful person of the week. Each of us said why we believed the person we chose was the most thoughtful. The thoughtfulness we were appreciating was often as simple as volunteering to help out with a chore or spending extra time with one of us. These weekly sessions reinforced thoughtfulness in the family.

Growing up with thoughtfulness as an important quality naturally makes our relationships stronger and it becomes part of the everyday way we treat others. To give without expecting anything in return is a fulfilling and self-reinforcing process. Can you remember when being thoughtful was rewarding, when it really felt good? Do you think of things to do with or for your mate that he or she would find especially pleasing? Thoughtfulness does not need to be elaborate. Sending a card in the mail, washing your partner's car, or surprising him or her with a special night out are thoughtful acts.

If for some reason the idea of being thoughtful makes you feel flat or empty or you have negative feelings or fears about being thoughtful, then it may be time to take an inventory, which includes doing an honest appraisal of your relationship. Have the two of you grown selfish and cold, which is the opposite of the original reasons you got together? Do you carry around unresolved conflict? Do you keep score, perhaps concluding, "She never [or he] never did _____, why should I?" Fill in the blank with what you use to keep score. When the desire to please your partner is diminished, consider that an early warning sign that your relationship needs attention.

Can you give or do for your partner without strings attached? This is an important question because thoughtfulness is one of the most satisfying ingredients in a love relationship. We see thoughtfulness in action with little looks, affirmative statements, touches, surprises, cards, letters, phone calls, meaningful talks, and setting aside time to be together and listen to each other's concerns. For busy parents, especially mothers, some practical actions are probably the most romantic kind of thoughtfulness.

Remembering Gratitude

THE COMMITMENT OR BOND

Dearest Brave One,

Thank you for sharing some time with me! It makes me dance through and through...like a line dance of a cowboy, the ballet of a ballerina, and the flying changes of a Lippizan stallion, all wrapped into the brightest feelings in the shape of a giant dancing heart, with a smile etched on it and the grace of God's love sprinkling gold dust all around.

Like thoughtfulness, gratitude is an important bond in relationships and strengthens its heart muscles. Is gratitude part of your relationships? In what ways do you let your partner know you are grateful? Have you spent less time lately thinking about the gratitude you have about your relationship? Gratitude means noticing the wonderful things about your relationship and rejoicing in them. It means acknowledging what you cherish and are thankful for. Perhaps you are grateful for specific traits or habits your partner has in abundance. Perhaps you are thankful for one special thing in your relationship because it gives you joy.

When I was married, I remember giving this card, "God's Porch," to my husband. It said: *"If I could sit across from God, I'd thank him for the glory of the morning and for starry skies. I'd thank him for the magic of a child's smile and for memories."* It goes on to express many other grateful thoughts and ends with, *"and most of all I'd thank God for lending me you."* How often do you feel that way in your relationship? I remember that, even in the toughest of times, I always found things I appreciated about my partner. Sometimes I was even more grateful when things were bad. Have you ever felt that way? When things are really, really difficult, do you realize how many things you like about your loved one?

When I coach couples, I have them make a gratitude list at the end of each day and exchange the list of things about their partner for which they are grateful. As a therapist, my mother used to say to clients, "Do you have trouble or are you just making trouble?" I believe you are making trouble if you remember all the bad and forget the good. Most of us do tend to get lazy and judgmental in our relationships, so closing the day with a gratitude moment is like saying your nightly prayers. Gratitude can be a great gift, and like a smile, it is contagious.

Compromise and Compassion

Some of the greatest intimacy in relationships is created by the willingness to see the other's heart, hold it in your hand, feel the person's feelings, and then be willing to bend. To be compassionate is to step outside your own ego and judgment to make the moment your partner is sharing with you pure, clean, and unattached to any other incident or moment you have experienced in the past. It is listening to your partner as if for the first time and offering a fresh, new, forgiving, and uncluttered mind. It is being fully present for your partner by listening to your partner's breath, words, and tones, and by noticing your partner's body language, spirit, and energy. In other words, it involves holding the communication with your partner in a space of love, being still in the here and now, with a selfless and yielding heart. That is compassion. And it feeds the spiritual muscles of the relationship.

Compromise involves compassionate caring, listening, and attentiveness to the discussion at hand and linking this with the desire to work out a way to address the needed change or transition in a supportive and mutually acceptable way.

Many heated arguments center around money, for example, and this issue calls for both compassion and compromise. Compassionate listening forges a pathway leading to understanding your partner's desires, needs, and values around money, even when you are challenged in the same areas. For example, she wants a new outfit for the charity ball and he thinks she ought to wear the one she wore last year—it is in perfect shape and she wore it only once. She thinks he ought to make do with the hunting gear he already has rather than spending money on new equipment. After all, she thinks, he is spending enough money going on the trip, and besides, he is leaving her with the kids.

On a scale of 1-10 how important is the argument? In five years are you going to remember that she bought a new dress and he got new hunting gear? If you let go of the control and let your partner meet his or her needs, the silent undertow of the relationship continues to evolve instead of getting stuck in petty things that in the long run don't really matter. Interestingly enough, there is another benefit to finding ways to compromise. Researchers at Emory University have found that cooperating with another person activates the pleasure centers of the brain, the same parts that are stimulated by rewards like food or money.

There are certain situations that can cause trouble and for which compromise is difficult. One partner buys "big-ticket" items you have not agreed upon. Or, one individual creates credit card debt through overspending and "under-saving." Sometimes a critical issue like money concerns comes up continuously, and you never get anywhere by discussing it, even though you both have been compassionate and willing to compromise. In these situations I recommend that you seek assistance through relationship coaching, counseling, conflict resolution, or a couples' seminar. *Do not* let any issue go unresolved because it will undermine your relationship.

WHEN THE END COMES—RENEWAL OR DEPARTURE, CONTINUED

Dearest Glowing Truth,

Your business in bankruptcy, my miscarriages, our counseling, our talking divorce...

What this means and how it feels is something that awakens endless images of my worst fears, my worst losses, my deepest defeats, and my greatest sorrows, all finding their way to my heart at the same time.

I trust I must not give into these feelings, but reach deeper into my soul to achieve the wisdom and insight to face this aspect of the journey alone, with courage and knowing I must not focus on the pain and disappointment, but rather on bettering myself... trusting God and being still enough to know the calling of these trials.

I live the serenity prayer for now:

Dear God, grant me the serenity to accept the things I cannot change, the courage to change the things I can, and the wisdom to know the difference.

Other Relationships

Children: Relationships with children require a great deal of giving and letting go. If you are the child's parent or major caretaker, the child will base most of his or her romantic relationship choices on the example you give. You provide the mirror in which your children see themselves.

Teens: Assuming you are the parent or guardian of teenagers, the key to dealing with them is turning over the control of decision making to them at a reasonable pace as their maturity warrants. Even though your teen will most likely challenge most of what you say, communication needs to become and remain open and regular, even when it is uncomfortable. It is also important that your interactions with your teen be grounded in thoughtful and consistent intention and unconditional love.

Singles: If you are a single, you must have a clear understanding of who you are and what needs you are trying to meet in each type of relationship. You are no different than partnered adults, and all the rules of relationship that apply to them apply to you.

Pets: Relating to pets is a two-way street. In other words, communication goes both ways. You will find pets are great communicators if you are willing to listen to them. For instance, if you pay attention to their cues, they will let you know when they want out, when they want to eat or when they want to be loved on. It is important to be clear about what your expectations in relation to your pet are and to then consistently convey them to your pet. The more consistent you are, the clearer the pet's understanding will be. For example, when you say "no," do you physically stop his behavior or do you continuously repeat the word no without making him stop, expecting him to understand without example? Mixed signals confuse and upset the communication with your pet.

Summary

There is no dancing spirit like the dance of love, which involves both commitment and total oneness. Growing, communicating, and letting unconditional love flow between people is the deepest passion, the greatest joy, and the heart's truest passage.

Spirit dances with anticipation and knows no greater joy than the union of spirits dancing as one.

— MELANEY SREENAN, PH.D.

Meditation

I recommend this as silent meditation with your partner. This can be a walking meditation or done lying down side-by-side or when sitting together. If you are lying down, remember to have the spine straight and the stomach free from restriction so your breath may come easily. With your partner, create an intention for this exercise, such as forgiveness, openness, deeper connection, or clarity on a particular issue. If you are doing this alone you can still choose an intention for the relationship. (If you are doing this as a walking meditation, then skip the "close your eyes section" and focus on the breathing section.)

Close your eyes. Choose an intention and breathe into the space you are in.

As you begin gently breathing, you may want to hold hands or have some part of your body touching your partner's body. Feel the energy between you and breathe into it. Send love and peace and harmony to your partner...smile and release the negative past...release all the tension that you may have as you come into this close space with your partner.

Go inside now and enter the deepest place of silence you can find. Quiet your mind and let go of all the thoughts and busyness you have in the way. Breathe. Slow down your energy and thoughts. Connect with the love you feel in your soul for the being inside you and the one next to you. Breathe into it and begin to expand the love...make it strong and big. Feed it more love and energy and give it life... imagine it as pure as the sunshine on a lake, as quiet and innocent as the fresh fallen snow, or as gentle as a leaf blowing slowly in the wind to the ground.

Now go to the intention that you have chosen...say it to yourself quietly. Begin a quiet inner conversation with your mate about this intention... write him or her a love letter in your heart. Let only positive words flow. Feel the love between you and your partner and let that guide your love letter response to the intention. Breathe three long, slow deep breaths into this love and your letter of intention. Deepen your feelings about this person and go more into the direction of the good in your mate and all that you love about him or her... imagine telling your mate what you adore and cherish and love about him or her. Spend a little more time in this loving space and bring your partner into it by feeling his or her presence in your space, by touching hands or hearing your mate's breath. Embrace the feelings of love and joy and partnership. Bring in any other positive thoughts you have and focus on them. Now thank your partner inside your heart for being such a precious being. Place all these feelings and thoughts in your heart and feel how big and joyous it feels. Breathe some slow, powerful, smiling breaths.

When you are ready, come back to your body, your space, and your partner. Breathe slowly back into this place with your partner and open your eyes. Turn to your partner and in silence, without words, communicate how much you love you feel. Spend several minutes silently communicating about your love.

Once you have completed this silent exercise, take ten minutes to write down all the things you love about your partner in love letter fashion starting with Dear ...and ending with Love... Now take turns reading these words out loud to each other. Make a habit of doing this meditation weekly.

Fieldplay

1. Make a list of things that take priority over your relationship. Decide what needs to be moved down or off the list in order to move your relationship to the top.

2. Describe your parents' relationship. Describe your own relationship. How are they different? How are they the same? List what insights on these lists can encourage growth.

3. List all the fears, resistance, or excuses you may have when you think about what could happen if you allow intimacy with your partner to reach a new level.

4. Talk to your partner about a time of day, every day, that you can talk or at least connect, even if it is walking in silence holding hands. Vow to make your relationship a priority for three months and see how it can expand your love and enhance other areas of your life.

Daily Play

1. Have your partner make a list of all the things he or she would love from you. These may be things like time, energy, listening, a weekend away, a card a week. Then do three of those things a month.

2. Create a place in the heart of your relationship to place gratitude and keep it alive. Feed it by being aware of and emphasizing the good in your partner. Show your partner what you are grateful for, no matter how small. Even in the worst of conflicts, you can still be grateful for your partner's red hair or soft skin or, hopefully, you can find much deeper things on a good day. Make a list, commit it to memory, and then promise to share several things on that list each day. Make a habit of telling your partner all the things you cherish and adore and appreciate about her or him.

3. Make this fun. Write a list of 50 things you could do for your partner; see how quickly you can complete the list.

4. Make a date to meet with your loved one for twenty minutes daily. Brainstorm about natural and creative ways to be together and enjoy and rediscover each other. Incorporate this into your daily life and it will become a habit.

Resources

My Lover, Myself: Self Discovery Through Relationship, David Kantor, Ph.D.; Penguin Putnam, 1999.

> *A well-known therapist puts in layperson's terms the keys to the couple achieving their highest potential.*

Spiritual Divorce, Debbie Ford; Harper Collins, 2001.

> *Divorce as a Catalyst for an Extraordinary Life. This book assists the reader in seeing the end of a marriage as steps to creating the life of your dreams.*

The Eden Project: In Search of the Magical Order, James Hollis; Inner City Books, 1998.

> *A Jungian perspective on relationship. Truly a thought provoking and challenging book on how to take personal responsibility for the relationships we are in. He asks us to grow individually rather than seek others to rescue us.*

Getting the Love You Want: A Guide for Couples, Harville Hendrix, Ph.D.; Harper Perennial Library, 1990.

In my opinion the best book on having a life long, fulfilling relationship. As a seasoned counselor, Hendrix gives sound advice on a long-lasting union.

The Couples Companion: Meditations and Exercises for Getting the Love You Want, Harville Hendrix; Simon & Schuster Trade, 1994.

This book offers to help readers, via meditations and healing exercises, recapture and expand upon the joyous and rewarding experience of a fulfilled relationship.

Finding Love, Harville Hendrix; Sounds True Incorporated, 1995.

A three cassette set in which Dr. Hendrix offers help for listeners who want to develop the skills they need to find the love of a lifetime. Single men and women can learn how to prepare for love and bring it into their lives.

Keeping the Love You Find: A Personal Guide, Harville Hendrix; Pocket Books, 1998.

Hendrix has developed a brilliant, thought-provoking, and innovative self-help program for single people who yearn for the pleasures and rewards of a loving relationship.

The Path to Love: Spiritual Strategies for Healing, Deepak Chopra; Three Rivers Press, 1998.

This is a wondrous journey...philosophical, inspiring, and ultimately very practical. This is a book that can change lives as it invites the spirit to work its wonders on the most complex and richly rewarding terrain of all: the human heart.

Homes of Honor and Love is a Decision Video Series, Dr Gary Smalley.

Dr. Smalley has a number of books on relationships as well as tape and video series on healthy families. Love is a Decision Video Series is a nine session series with a workbook to do with the whole family or a group. To order 1-800-84 TODAY.

CHAPTER 7

CLEAR THE WAY

Spirit taught me to give the impossible a chance.

— MELANEY SREENAN, PH.D.

Spirit needs a container to pour itself into. Grace needs an arena in which to incarnate. Waiting can be such a place, if we allow it.

When the Heart Waits

— SUE MONK

It is said that the two most important gifts you can give your child are roots and wings. How are your roots? How solid is your foundation? And are you using your wings? As a teen I resisted the big leap into independence that leaving home required. With a strong tone in her voice and a look of determination mixed with empathy, my mother said, "Gosh darn it, Melaney, I am going to push you out of this nest if that's the last thing I do." It was time for me to spread my wings and leave the nest.

Even if you had a tough childhood, you may not have completely left the nest. You know this is the case if you still live according to many of the rules you learned in childhood. Physically leaving home does not necessarily mean you have gained spiritual and emotional independence. This is true especially with major life themes such as money, career, and relationships.

From birth to age six we gather knowledge about the outside world in relation to ourselves. During this time, the developing personality sends out feelers to the world to see if the conditions around it are favorable or unfavorable. For some people, the feelers come back with flashing red lights, shouting "Warning! Warning! Don't go there!" For others, the feelers come back with a message of warmth, safety and peace. In this friendly situation, the message is, "Go out and be you."

By age two, most of us have all the information we need to determine whether we are safe and the world is a good place to be, or that we are not safe and it's necessary to adopt an "us against them" attitude. This process is usually complete by age six. If you are lucky enough to reach age six and believe you are safe and the world is a wonderful place, then you have a great start in life—an incredible foundation. This foundation fosters your potential to move quickly to the next level of personal development.

The next phase of development occurs between ages six and twelve. This is the time you spend exploring society through the reflection of the mirror your family has given you. If your mirror reflects the image of a great person, then your six-year-old mind generalizes and accepts that everyone in the world loves you and wants the best for you. At this stage you turn to your world—the larger society—to provide answers and fulfill your need to be liked and be a part of the tribe outside of your family.

Because the social self is developing, these years can be challenging, even for those whose families have given them a strong foundation. During this developmental phase you can pick up momentum to move forward or you can be devastated and held back by the smallest thing. This depends on how sensitive you are and how much you look to the world to fill you up. Many things influence the developing social self: being laughed at by a peer, treatment by teachers, shifts in the family dynamics, including the birth of a sibling, parental marital problems, a move, the loss of a grandparent, or the death of a pet. An off-hand remark can throw you, or a classroom experience can embarrass you. You may fail in a sport or in an extracurricular activity. These incidents, though they can seem small when you describe them, have the potential to cause you to question your social foundation.

When negative interactions or events occur at this stage, you may walk away from the experience with some negative self-talk, which at the time may be designed to protect you from being vulnerable and hurt again. For example, you may have a teacher who thinks you are too hyper, energetic, and enthusiastic. You thought this behavior was good because your family reinforced that idea. But now a teacher gives you a new message and intentionally or unintentionally negatively influences you. In response, you vow to yourself that you will not be so outgoing in class or enthusiastically answer questions ever again. Should this message occur again and again, it can evolve to a deeper idea. For example, rather than being vivacious and energetic, you come to believe you are annoying. If the message continues, the idea can grow deeper roots and before long you believe that no one likes you and you may begin to think you are unlovable.

Typically, you adjust to the developing beliefs about yourself and don't check them out with anyone. Your self-talk sounds like this: I'm annoying, no one likes me, and I'm too hyper. In large part, our history determines how we will process these external messages, this outside information. Much of this self-concept development occurs on an unconscious level and unless we bring these negative feelings to the conscious mind and face the fear they engender, they will delay our transition to the next level of our higher-self functioning.

A Conversation with Fear

A series of interactions that result in negative assumptions may lead to putting coping tools in place that can create an endless cycle of defense. If your self-worth is sabotaged by negative judgments created in your childhood, it is time to review the memories surrounding the experiences that led you to accept the negative judgments of others as your own. Most likely, these memories have been "hiding out." You are left with the result and the cause of your negative self-talk seems far-removed. As you review memories from childhood, a general feeling of fear may surface. For example, you may be afraid of rejection because you feel you are not lovable. Paradoxically, the fear you do not address will likely continue to interfere with the foundation of who you are and the way you think about yourself.

Let's say you're in college and you have not addressed your unconscious fear of success. This feeling is unconscious so quite naturally you aren't in touch with it. However, after you identify that you are afraid of success, it may be possible to trace its origin back to a time when you were given negative feedback and made fun of by your peers. You want to be a physician, you have a great G.P.A., and an Ivy League medical school accepted you. You're elated, but a part of you hears the fearful voice of your past undermining your ability to fulfill the dream of completing medical school. During the first semester you socialize a lot, do the party scene, and consequently feel too tired to study. Sometimes you even sleep through your classes, saying you'll get the notes from others.

This behavior is the "You will never amount to anything!" message at work, and unintentionally you are sabotaging your dreams. This hidden belief manifests itself in a form that proves the message right. As long as you remain unaware of what is at work in your life, it will continue to control you and, most likely, destroy your dreams. This kind of hidden belief can take on a life and power that is all its own, thereby causing you to fulfill its goal, which is self-defeat. On the other hand, once you understand the root cause of your fear of success, you can heal the distorted pieces of your self-concept and move on.

Almost everything we think or have derived about ourselves that is negative can be traced back to fear. Your objective is to choose the opposite, love. So, to resolve the cycle of self-defeat is to ask yourself what you are afraid of and then trace it back to the message or survival decision you made in childhood. Acknowledge the fear, break it down into sizable chunks, and work each piece of the underlying emotion until you get to acceptance or love.

Do you need to fall in love with yourself? Addressing your fears is a grand place to start that process.

Old Thoughts and Well-meaning Friends

We come to maturity with negative and limiting beliefs formed in childhood. These limitations can come from a number of sources and we may be unaware of those that are deepest and most ingrained. Some beliefs may be generational in that they are passed down to us from our parents and may have roots many generations ago. A parent with low self-esteem believes he or she is not good enough and that belief can be transferred to you unintentionally. Friends, coaches, teachers, or ministers may pass on their limiting beliefs as well. We all have influences that can be traced to community or societal beliefs.

If you have trouble identifying your limiting beliefs or their origins you might want to review Chapter 3 to see if you can discover the origin of your limiting beliefs in your disrespect tapes.

Trying or Doing

Believing in yourself and getting out of your own way takes consistent attention.

Trying to believe in yourself will never get the job done. In elementary school we got grades for our efforts. Back then, trying counted. I could never understand why students got A's for effort but D's in the class, meaning that they received rewards for trying, even when they did not fulfill the requirements of the class.

Your path will not be paved as long as you imagine yourself "winning" good grades for trying. The concept is quite pervasive in our society. I will *try* to get that project completed. I will *try* to improve grammar. I will *try* to be less judgmental.

We all are skilled at making excuses for ourselves about why we don't have the life, the job, or the relationship we want, and it can usually be traced back to "I tried—I really did." Trying lacks commitment. It lacks integrity. Trying lacks power. How do you feel when you hear someone say, "I'll try to make it" or "I'll try to remember?" Do you feel a positive charge or a negative one? Trying is often empty—it is a zero on the energy scale.

As for your spirit dances process, the only way to validate your own journey is through being fully energized and completely committed to it. Doing, rather than trying to do, is one of the crucial steps for reaching the next level of development. Taking that stand of determined doing and putting it into action draws from the faith, courage, and authenticity you have developed through this course. Create it. Make it come alive. Stay away from anything that reduces the energy to move forward and complete your objective. Do the work of spirit. It will strengthen your foundation and springboard you into reaching the next level of wherever you are going. Doing is the way to bring something more vibrant, alive, and powerful to your being.

Focus and Guidelines

We are coming to the final stages of this spirit journey. Now is the time to focus on what needs to move out of the way in order for your best life to develop and function. When we focus on what really matters and stay unwavering, things begin to shift. You have gained great insight into who you are through the self-discovery process of the earlier chapters of this book. When you focus on what you want, your life, including your relationships, will be different. In order to move into a new phase of your life, you must sink your teeth into what is in the way and put time and energy into clearing the path of unnecessary obstacles—the old limiting beliefs are part of the debris you need to sweep away. You know you're in the right place if you feel energized, joyful, and hopeful as you focus on authentic and clearly defined goals.

At this point, it's important that you review lessons you have learned, insights you have obtained, and create guidelines for the next three months. These guidelines are meant to serve you as you move along your path. They will give you clarity, energy, and courage. Guidelines should be simple and direct: "I choose to believe in myself" is a direct statement, not a goal or an item on your "To Do List." Guidelines are what you need to know in order to support yourself through the next three months. While writing this book, my guideline was "Lighten Up." Clients have chosen guidelines like "Smile," "Bring Joy," "Laugh," "Stay Focused," or "Manifest Abundance." The guideline choices you make give you an angel on your shoulder that whispers in your ear and keeps you on the right path. These guidelines are your friends and strength as you get closer and closer to your authentic life plan.

If your guidelines give you power and energy, and make you feel clear, courageous, and whole, you will know you are heading in the right direction.

Naming It All—All You Love

Naming all you love is the fun step in this chapter. This is a time for telling your practical mind to take a vacation, or at least a nap. This is heart stuff, clear and pure. Deep down, what do you want to claim in this lifetime? What might be unfathomable or seemingly out of reach, but is yours to address and fantasize about? Draw close to your dreams and let spirit dance around you. Now what is it you truly dream of—we're talking about the big stuff here. When you close your eyes and the dance of the heart takes you to magical places, what do you see and feel? You may want to practice this daily.

For most people, engaging in expansive dreams represents a huge stride toward living their imagined life, but it is a necessary and worthwhile one. Some people find it easiest to do this exercise early in the morning while they are still half-asleep. They can get to heart dancing places and jot down thoughts before the head totally engages and moves to thoughts of the day. In this "between worlds" state the spirit has a better chance of playing with the dream of your heart. Begin to shift your thoughts to having your dreams come true. Own your thoughts about your dreams. Give them life and energy. Feel the power of your passions and your dreams of the ultimate life you are in the process of designing.

Stepping Into Your Power

The act involved with claiming your power partners well with the clarity of the perfect life you design for yourself. This is a time of truly looking in the mirror and seeing negative things standing around you, beside you, on top of you, and in front of you. These negative beliefs and patterns of thinking crush your dreams, give you pain and discomfort, and stop you from breaking free. The picture of the majestic stallion rearing up and striking out is an idea you can visualize as you step into your power. What thinking is keeping you in stories about yourself that lock up your spirit? What is stopping you from truly being yourself? What keeps you looking down versus looking ahead? How and where do you lack confidence and clarity? What allows your spirit to flourish and what shows up to stop you now? Review the internal tapes of limiting beliefs. Look at the strongest, most powerful, limiting belief or behavior that goes against you as you reach out for the divine life. Explore every nook and cranny—look far and wide, dig deep.

Check out your tolerations and belief and value systems. Notice the people watching you from the sidelines and question what you're doing. Notice those along side you and those that want to hold you back.

Take a close look at your power. What does it say to you? What do you most struggle with as you reach for the powerful mustang within you that rears towards the sky? Stepping into your power may feel risky but when you experience the great energy within you, you will know you have made the right choice.

It is time to cut loose! Shine! Be all that you were put here to be!

Summary

Know that spirit is calling you to live passionately. The highest truth is passionately being all you can be. If you can imagine it, you can achieve it. Let your dancing spirit do the rest of the work.

Spirit beckons the wildest dancing energy to explode with life's passion.

— MELANEY SREENAN, PH.D.

Meditation

Get into your quiet space. Slowly begin to fall into the quiet and peaceful garden of your being. Relaxing more and more. Letting go of all the thoughts and images that fill your mind, just breathe into the peace and knowing of your heart center. Focus on your breath, listening to the slow in and out like a gentle ocean wave. Quieter and quieter. Deeper and deeper. Check your body for any tension or worry and let it go by breathing into it. Focus on clear, calm, peaceful, warm light and loving light. When you are ready go to the door of your garden and before passing through the door, check any energy drains or self doubt at the door. Take a deep, long, loving breath as you enter your peaceful, safe garden. Notice the sounds and the smells and the sensations of your special place. Feel the ease, comfort, and security of your garden. Sit down in a comfortable and warm space in your garden and slowly, lovingly go back to the time you were age six. What were you doing? Who was there? What did they think about you? What really made you happy? Feel the feelings of that time and age. Embrace the answers and the questions that arise as you explore this area of your life. How does it feel to be six years old? Who loves you? How do they show that you are important to them? What are your main sources of love? What are your main sources of doubt? Sit across from your six-year-old self and ask any questions you believe would help you know and seek your higher intelligence and ask your child what you need most to let go of. Sit with this six-year-old you and just notice the eyes and the heart and the soul. Just be silent and listen and watch. Give yourself a few minutes to just BE with this part of you, this part of your life. Breathing...appreciating, enjoying, embracing, feeling, touching...breathing.

Now when you are ready, thank your little child for visiting and for the wisdom and answers he or she has given you and take the love, union, and peace and place it upon your heart and your lips. Kiss this precious being farewell for now and slowly get up from your special place and move toward the door of your garden. Pick a flower or some special symbol to bring with you as a reminder of this journey into your soul self. Remember that you can return to this place at any time. Trust you will remember all that was given to you here and that you will use it in a way that is empowering and peaceful.

When you are ready, come back to this room, this space, this time and write about your experience and the answers to the questions in the meditation.

You can do this meditation every day for the rest of the week and see what answers you get.

Fieldplay

1. Who was most influential person in your daily life when you were six years old and what was he or she like? What rules did this person live by and how were these rules imparted or imposed on you?

2. What is your life purpose?

4. What brings you passion? Sometimes it's easier to list things that destroy your passion.

- Pick the top five limiting beliefs that influence your life the most now.

- Write down how they protected you as a child.

- Write how they hinder you and hold you back as an adult.

5. Now make a commitment this week to address each one of limiting beliefs starting with the easiest one first. Use a 21-day-plan in which you do something specific and measurable each day, taking less than five minutes, for 21 days to overcome this limiting belief. Do this with each limiting belief.

6. If you were living the perfect life, what would it look like?

Daily Play

Revisit your description of your perfect life—integrate one aspect of your perfect life into your life daily.

Resources

52 Ways to Simplify Your Life, Lynn Gordon; Chronicle Books, 1997.

From a few quiet moments alone to basic methods for losing clutter such as getting off junk mail lists, here are 52 smart and simple ways to ease life's hectic pace. Ideal for anyone looking for peace of mind.

The Seat of the Soul, Gary Zukav; Fireside Books, 1998.

This book addresses the aspects of the soul, the inner you.

A Path with Heart: A Guide Through the Perils and Promises of Spiritual Life, Jack Kornfield; Bantam Doubleday Dell Pub, 1993.

This book uses the teachings of Buddha with humor and lightness, and addresses how to meditate and practice inner transformation.

Excuse Me, Your Life is Waiting, Lynn Grabhorn; Hampton Roads, 2000.

An encouraging and funny, yet serious, book about the astonishing power of feelings and why we don't achieve our dreams.

Life Makeovers, Cheryl Richardson; Broadway Books, 2000.

This book is a 52 week program for improving your life one week at a time.

Dark Side of the Light Chasers: Reclaiming Your Power, Creativity, Brilliance and Dreams, Debbie Ford; Riverhead Books, New York, New York, 1998.

A brilliant book by my favorite author on the keys to wholeness and transformation.

Love is Letting Go of Fear, Gerald Jampolsky; Celestial Arts, 1988 Revised Edition.

Based on material from "A Course in Miracles." This book teaches us how to let go of fear and how to remember that our very essence is love. Included are daily exercises that give a direct and effective method to bringing about individual transformation.

CHAPTER 8

MAKE YOUR WILDEST DREAMS COME ALIVE

Spirit taught me to dance with my feet off the ground.

— MELANEY SREENAN

"*Creativity flourishes not in certainty but in questions. Growth germinates not in tent dwelling but in upheaval. Yet, the seduction is always security rather than venturing, instant knowing rather than deliberate waiting.*"

When the Heart Waits

— SUE MONK

It's time to raise the bar and go to the next level! Now is the time to honor the divine self that you are meant to be and put yourself at the top of your priority list. Start this process by saying no to new demands or projects that distract you from the path of your divine self. Let people close to you know that for now you are going to focus on this transition. Trust that this focus will benefit everyone around you. Nothing and no one is more radiant and loving than individuals living their wildest dreams. Consider the possibility that you will resist doing this work. After all, it is much easier to shrink back and keep other things and people in the forefront than it is to take on this challenge and make yourself your top priority. Claiming our fullest lives may feel too risky.

Making room for the authentic life takes a strong commitment to yourself. However, the sooner you embrace this powerful theme the more you will see your life unfold in truly magical ways. Notice any inner resistance or dialogue that tempts you to hold back from the demands of this shift. Let the internal whispers go or write them down and see that these messages are grounded in fear or excuses. Remember you are here for a purpose. This is your chance to go after the best of yourself and the best of life. This is the place from which you make your most powerful contributions and your most profound experiences.

It takes energy to put yourself first and strive to be the best you can be. But I can assure you that if you step into the demands of this chapter you will have more than enough energy to continue your process. Be careful not to shrink back from this dynamic work; it holds the key to helping your spirit come alive.

We must be willing to get rid of the life we've planned, so as to have the life that is waiting for us.

— JOSEPH CAMPBELL

Pathways for a Passionate Life

I know a woman who has lived her life with purpose and passion despite many obstacles. Her passion was animals, children, and nature. A child of a multi-millionaire, she grew up in a household with live-in maids. Her life looked easy, but she contracted polio. She spent much of her childhood struggling to overcome the physical handicaps caused by the disease. In the 1940s, this intelligent woman completed college in three years with honors. While finishing her degree she fell in love with and married the college's top athlete and International Collegiate Boxer who went on to achieve a law degree. Before she married, she had never had to wash a dish or make a bed, but her dream was to live on a farm.

Eventually, this woman had nine children. She continued to love animals, children, and nature; others could see and feel her passion for these things. At some point, her husband became an abusive alcoholic. Despite the difficulty, she kept her passion and her purpose to rear and nurture her children and be the best she could be.

While she was pregnant with her ninth child her husband divorced her. She relied on her faith, her purpose, and her passion to survive the years after the divorce. She and her nine children, along with nine dogs and four horses, moved from the Mid-west to Florida to pursue graduate school. While working on her Ph.D. she made herself available to her children day and night. She made sure her children were surrounded by their beloved animals and immersed in nature. They were all very close and did everything together from horseback riding to tennis to studying. Her purpose and passion shined through her eyes and were reflected in the well-being of her children—her passion still shines to this day. She truly achieved balance in a life filled with purpose and she did it with passion. Without her passion she could not have overcome the obstacles along the way.

As you no doubt know, this woman is my mother. Today she lives in nature on a lake with seven acres and thirty miniature horses. Now, her grandchildren come to "Mimi's" to immerse themselves in nature, the animals, and her love.

Examining Your Purpose

Everyone has a purpose and is living it out whether they know it or not. Purpose includes both being and doing. Awareness of your purpose provides a foundation from which to make decisions and creates consistency in your life. Somehow things come together when you give language to your purpose.

For example, my personal purpose is to do the work of spirit, to listen to my mind, and to follow my heart and soul. With every person I encounter I want to give peace, harmony, happiness, and love. My purpose is to live a productive, soulful life. In business, my purpose is to inspire and facilitate the growth of those with whom I come into contact and to make a difference in their lives by offering my energy, insight, resources and, most of all, unconditional love.

Sometimes something very earth-shattering has to happen to us in order for us to look at our lives and visit our passion.

Sometimes it's the very frustration of our stumbling that provides us with the detour we need to get back on track toward our authenticity. Stop limiting Spirit. Work with Divine Intelligence and be grateful that God doesn't think like us."

Something More

— SARAH BAN BREATHNACH

Even with a Ph.D. in psychology and training in marriage counseling, I found myself ending a ten-year marriage and facing shattered dreams and promises. I realized that I must face myself on a new level in order to reconnect with my purpose and renew my passion with life.

It was my attraction to nature and the outdoors that brought me back to my life's passion. As Sarah Ban Breathnach says, "Passion is truth's soulmate." Where is passion in your life?

> *"My soul can find no staircase to Heaven unless it be through Earth's loveliness."*
>
> — MICHELANGELO

The Challenge of Priorities

My coaching clients often complain that life is moving so fast they can't seem to keep up. Their "to do lists" are never ending and sometimes checking half the items off the list is the biggest satisfaction of their day. Then, more items must be added and they're back in the same place. The same scenario repeats, day in and day out. Sound familiar? These lives are out of balance and are lived in a "get through" mode. Get through the list, the next board meeting, the morning, this week, and on and on. Clearly, when we live this way we are not connected with our purpose or our passion.

If you were to write your epitaph today what would it look like? "Here lies Sally. She proudly crossed off all the items on her "To Do" list" or "Rest his soul, John was always in a hurry" or "Peace be to Pat for she never got it right." In a culture that promotes more is better thinking, we get so caught up in the frenzied pace, we lose ourselves.

We are all given the twenty-four hours in a day. Look at the categories on the chart on the following page. If you were to fill in the spaces, what proportions would you get? Are you in or out of balance? To have a life with purpose and passion you must have balance.

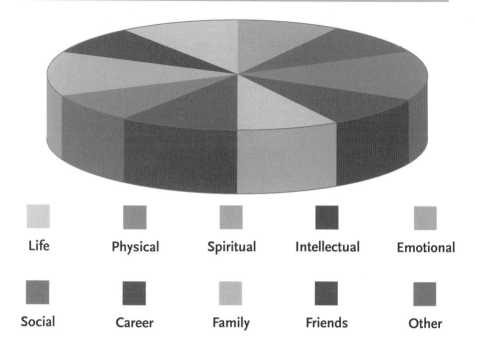

Life	Physical	Spiritual	Intellectual	Emotional
Social	Career	Family	Friends	Other

Passport to Life's Passion

I believe that your capacity for passion lives in your heart. When you discover your passion, you have uncovered the heart's deepest desires. When I lost my vision—my purpose and my passion—I knew I had lost myself in the process of trying to save my relationship. Ultimately, I found these missing parts of myself in the snow, in the darkness of the short mountain days, in the eyes of the deer and the elk, and in the eagles I watched daily. I found it when I examined the fear of thinking I'd starve to death while snowed in. I recovered my life's purpose by learning to drive the mountain roads in the snow and ice, despite avalanche warnings that kept even the locals from venturing out. I found it in learning to trust God again. Discover your passion by doing the work of spirit, listening to your head, and following your heart.

"dance as though no one is watching you,
love as though you have never been hurt before,
sing as though no one can hear you,
live as though heaven is on earth."

— SOUZA

Two of the things that energize my passion are dancing and loving, be it a child, a fresh breeze, a precious flower, or a significant other.

"One way to live your life is to struggle every step of the way
and then get it right in the last five minutes"

— ANONYMOUS

Exploring Your Values—Again

What are your authentic values? You made your list of values in Chapter 2, but how do they look to you now? Are they authentic? Are they aligned with your purpose, passion, and priorities? Wise teachers like Thomas Leonard and Wayne Dyer say that discomfort and strife come from being out of sync with your true values. Now is the time to take your life seriously. You are responsible for your happiness and you alone can make sure your values and priorities are aligned with your passion and purpose.

One of my values and priorities is achieving a balanced life. I have supported this priority by not scheduling appointments on Fridays in order to leave room for other things in my life. One of my clients said, "Gee, it must be nice to be off on Fridays."

"Well yes," I said, "I take a great deal of responsibility for my well-being, and this is one of the ways that I provide balance in my life."

My client was miffed when she left my office, but several months later she had integrated the practice of taking one day off a week in her own life.

So, are the values you wrote several weeks ago still valid? Remember that our values drive us internally and to be truly authentic, our values must resonate and align with our purpose and passion. Since they are at the core of our nature, they mirror the depth of our spirits. When we honor our values, they give us energy.

One of my strongest values is freedom. As a child I had no idea I was operating on that value when I insisted on riding horses even though I had been forbidden to do so because I had a seizure disorder with blackouts and blind spells. I would create ways to be free to ride my horse. I found ways to freely enjoy riding my horse, such as riding in the night of a full moon, although night riding was forbidden. This expression of freedom allowed my passion to get the charge it needed to refresh and lift my spirit.

Goals Along Your Path

As you mature and have some say in how your journey unfolds, you develop the ability to create goals. Like baking a cake, too much of one ingredient or not enough of another can make a big difference in the outcome. If you don't know what you are after, you will get only what comes along. If you want special or specific things out of life, you must plan a course for getting them.

My parents were my main role models for goal setting. My father always told me that you get out of life what you put into it. My mom always told me that God never gives you more than you can handle. Boy, did I think they went to the wrong school. My mother's goal was to earn a Ph.D. in psychology, and she accomplished her goal, even though it seemed she already had way too much to handle, what with nine kids, a farm, animals, and other responsibilities, plus being on her own. It seemed to me that she exaggerated about God never giving us more than we could handle. In fact, it sounded to me like a luxury belief—one that only the rich could afford, just as it's easy to say that money's not everything when you have plenty of it.

The cold, muddy, rainy afternoon my mom was served with divorce papers, I was elated. So were my brothers and sisters. My mother cried, but given the atmosphere in the household prior to this final step, it seemed as if we were given total freedom. It gave me a chance to let go of trying to be in control of every situation I encountered. Before my family situation changed, I always anticipated what would happen next, trying to react and create the outcome, but of course, that was an illusion. I was never in control in the first place, and I always felt as if I failed to reach my goal.

My mistake was creating a goal that involved controlling a situation that was not in my power to change. A true goal involves something that is about *you*. You can manage and control your actions, but not someone else's. This is true freedom and it is the fuel that allows us to create authentic goals.

As I recall, no one in my household talked about goals and their influence on our life's journey; but goals were evident in all that my parents had accomplished throughout the years. My mother wanted to finish college before she married, so she crammed four years of study into three. She wanted to live in the country, although that meant leaving behind her privileged life in a mansion, complete with maids. Dad' s goal was to be wealthy, even if it meant long years of law school and going into the service to pay for it. In addition, he wanted lots of kids, even if that meant he'd have to work longer hours to afford them.

Nowadays, most of us talk about the tradeoffs we're willing to make and the deep desires we have in terms of goals. Many parents encourage their children to think in terms of goals and the steps needed to reach them. Past generations might have said, "I want to go to college and I'm willing to work after school and all summer to earn the money to go." This generation is likely to say, "My goal is to go to the University of _____ and I'll need x number of dollars. So, my first goal is to get a job paying x amount of money, of which I will save 80 percent... ." You get the idea.

Many people, the younger generation included, create goals while they are young and need a foundation to begin a career or a life path. But they drop the concept with the diploma or first job or their first good promotion. They forget that creating goals serves us throughout life because goals help us live consciously and with purpose.

Goals support us in many ways. They give us energy, focus and clarity. With each role you have in your life you have some goals whether they are acknowledged by your conscious mind or not. In order for goals to be effective they must be aligned with your values, your purpose, and your passion. Goals must be specific and measurable. So if your goal is to learn to speak Spanish or lose weight, this leaves a great deal to the imagination. A goal you can measure is to sign up for a weekly Spanish class for the next eight weeks. This is your first step. Wanting to lose weight is a vague concept, but putting a plan in motion to lose ten pounds by October 1 by eating three nutritionally balanced meals a day and walking for 45 minutes five days a week has the "feel" of a goal. Maybe the first steps are even smaller, i.e., researching Spanish classes or consulting with a nutritionist to learn about serving portions and meal plans.

Having goals involves taking a risk. I believe that avoiding risk has a numbing affect on us. Taking risks is necessary if you are to fulfill the vision of your spirit and the quest of your soul.

Do you feel numb or flat about your life? Are you living day to day just to get by? Can you remember the last time you took a risk? What was the outcome? What attitudes and habits do you have in place that support you in avoiding risk? Committing to a goal or dream requires that you take a certain amount of risk to achieve it. When I say we must take risks, I don't mean taking a risk just for the sake of it. I mean taking a risk with your vision in mind. Do you need to do something that seems risky? Identify what you are avoiding.

As I said earlier, my vision and my soul's quest was to live in the mountains. One winter day I stepped into the risk and moved in the direction of my dream. It involved leaving the security of an established home and professional practice. My colleagues called my decision to leave for the mountains "professional suicide." However, once I decided to take the journey towards my dream, the energy of my soul's vision and the clarity of the goals that had been in my head since childhood overcame my fear of the unknown. In other words, my desire had more energy than my fear, the risk seemed acceptable, and obstacles were manageable. Not knowing where I would land was less frightening because I was comforted by the determination of my soul. Risks are an essential part of the process of determining and attaining goals.

Goals support what really resonates for you. What is the big, juicy fantasy life that is meant for you? If you were to take your happiness seriously, what goals would you put in place? Once you accept that you create your destiny, what would cause you to postpone going after your goal? You are the one that will look back on your life and feel the satisfaction or the disappointment. You hold the key to the ultimate life. Do you know what your dream life looks like and what goals you need to put in place to guide your journey to this fulfilling life?

At some point or another, most of us bury our passion and purpose somewhere in the mountain of all the obligations and "shoulds" we impose on ourselves. These types of situations aren't hopeless. There is no time like right now to stop holding back, to push through your resistance, fears and excuses, and open to all that is yours for the taking.

Summary

Spirit calls you to awaken to the deepest purpose and passion within you. Spirit waits for you to dance in the sunlight with all the freedom your heart can hold. Come join spirit! Spirit waits for you at the edge of knowing where being all that you can be is the way of life. Purpose, passion, values, goals, and risks balanced delicately create the dancing profound spirit of happiness and a complete life. Between the internal and external resources that are yours for the seeking, you have everything you need to allow your deepest passion to unfold.

*Spirit sprinkles golden freedom and truth as you dance to all
the love you are.*

— MELANEY SREENAN, PH.D.

Meditation

Get into your quiet space with your journal beside you. Imagine yourself with each breath sinking deeper and deeper into the passion of your life. Slowing down, becoming more and more peaceful and relaxed. Breathing in, one, clearer, calmer closer to your purpose. Breathing out, letting go, clearing your mind, freeing your spirit. Breathing all the way out until there is no more breath left in you. Breathing in, two, full confident, strong and insightful. Breathing out fear, resistance, old habits. Breathing in, three, passion, purpose, priorities, goals. Breathing out doubt, old tapes, questioning. Sinking deeper and deeper into the truth of your passion. More and more quiet and peaceful. Breathing out fear anxiety and worry. Down deeper and deeper. Breathing in, going down more and more. More purpose, passion, clarity, authenticity. Breathing out negative thoughts and self-doubt. Down more and more reaching closer and closer to the garden of your passion. Connecting with spirit more and more. When you are ready, go to the private garden of your spirit. After relaxing here and taking in the smells, sights, and sounds of this spirit place, invite spirit to join you. Ask this soulful self what it needs most from you in order to carry you to the next level. Sit silently and wait for the answer. Breathe slowly and purposefully. Listen and honor everything you hear even if it doesn't make any sense. Look at spirit. Notice spirit's face and eyes. Let the expressions of spirit give you courage and insight. Let this great energy give you all the information you are searching for. Embrace this aspect of yourself as you invite more open communication and understanding. Sink into the quiet union with this guide you have and feel yourself just being there. Be there. Breathe. Invite. Feel. Unite.

Ask spirit any other questions that you may have. Questions such as, How do I get where I am going? What will be there along the way to support me? How will I know that I am doing the right thing? Sit silently and trust that the answer will come. Look around at the precious garden of your soul and invite any other wisdom or input you may need along this part of the journey. Breathe. Be patient. Let it flow. Try to not make sense out of all of it. The answers may come to you in the form of pictures, imagines, words, sensations, colors, or stories. Imagine slow, easy, gentle, giving, receiving, growing, trust, faith and knowing. Let the information flow

Slowly and gently, when you feel you have all the information you came here for, thank your spirit guide for the time and wisdom. Gradually come back to the room, trying not to come out of the space you are in. Pick up your journal and with your non-dominant hand write the answer to the question about what spirit needs most from you in order to carry you to the next level. Just put the pen to the paper and write. Do not censor or review the writing. Let it happen. Again this information may come to you in sensations, words, images, stories. You may get one word answers or examples may simply show up. Trust you are getting the information you need and go with it. Write it. Draw it. Do whatever spirit directs you to do.

While still in this meditative place write the answers to the questions in Fieldplay. You can use your writing (dominant) hand for this if you prefer.

"Each moment in time we have it all even when we think we don't."

Lessons of Love

— MELODY BEATTIE

"Money, marital status, fame, admiration, and accomplishment mean nothing if the soul is starving."

Something More

— SARAH BAN BREATHNACH

Fieldplay

1. What would your pie chart (as illustrated in this chapter) look like if you were living your life on purpose right now? (Refer to the pie chart presented earlier in this chapter.) Some areas to consider are physical, spiritual, intellectual, emotional, social, career, familial, friends, financial, and relational. You may have other areas that are important to you as well. Take one area of your life at a time and see how it feels to try on the ideal life—a life with purpose and passion in that particular aspect of your life. See what happens. Are areas of your life perfect for you right now? What are they?

2. What are your twenty strongest wishes?

3. List ten goals or ideal wishes you have in each of the following areas:

> Emotional life, social life, financial life, spiritual life, physical life, familial life, intellectual life, and relational life. Rank them in order of importance.

4. Do the same for your professional goals. List them and then rank them.

5. List your top 20 values from Chapter 2.

"It you're not standing at the edge you are taking up too much space."

— EUNICE AZZANI, EXECUTIVE VICE-PRESIDENT
KORN/FERRY INTERNATIONAL

"Each moment in time we have it all even when we think we don't."

Lessons of Love

— MELANEY BEATTIE

Daily Play

1. Revisit your passion. Define what it is and set specific goals to achieve a balance with your passion.

2. Be the leading lady or gentleman of your life and your work. Be all that you can be with purpose and passion.

Resources

Real Magic: Creating Miracles in Everyday Life, Wayne Dyer; Harper, 1992.

This book is inspiring and has great examples and an easy-to-follow format on how to attain your highest vision.

Life Strategies: Doing What Works - Doing What Matters, Phillip McGraw; Hyperion, 1999.

Guides the reader to understanding of growing through 10 life laws.

The Heart of the Soul: Emotional Awareness, Gary Zukav and Linda Francis; Simon and Schuster, 2002.

Combines spirituality and psychology to deepen the understanding of the whole person and creation of authentic power.

The Way of the Wizard, Deepak Chopra; Harmony Books, 1995.

Contains 20 Spiritual Lessons for people to us to create a better life.

Take Time for Your Life: A Personal Coach's Seven-Step Program for Creating the Life You Want, Cheryl Richardson; Broadway Books, 1999.

Personal coach Cheryl Richardson helps people create the lives they want. In Take Time for Your Life, she shows you how to switch from being stressed, unfulfilled, and overworked, to "living a life you love" by using a seven-step process.

Stand Up for Your Life: Develop the Courage, Confidence, and Character to Fulfill Your Greatest Potential, Cheryl Richardson; Free Press, 2002.

Stand Up for Your Life urges readers to stop playing it safe by putting their needs and priorities aside. Her premise: by spending less time listening to others and more time strengthening your relationship with yourself, you can learn to govern your own life and influence others.

The Way of the Peaceful Warrior: A Book That Changes Lives, Dan Millman; Starseed Press, 1984.0

This bestseller is based on the story of a champion gymnast who, guided by a powerful old warrior, journeys into realms of romance and magic.

Sacred Journey of the Peaceful Warrior, Dan Millman; Starseed Press, 1991.

The author provides his readers with perennial wisdom and guidance for life, as he shares his adventures on the first steps of his sacred journey.

Everyday Enlightenment: The Twelve Gateways to Personal Growth, Dan Millman; Warner Books, Incorporated, 1999.

Dan Millman tells listeners how to see the spiritual in everyday life.

CHAPTER 9

CREATE YOUR LIFE PLAN

Spirit taught me to make friends with shadow or it will spook you.
— MELANEY SREENAN, PH.D.

*Do not go where the path may lead, go instead where there is no
path and leave a trail.*
— RALPH WALDO EMERSON

This chapter is your action plan for living your dream life. It is your
opportunity to create the clarity that will propel you into the world of
your dreams.

When we started this journey, I made a promise to you. I said that if you
worked with the book's ideas and followed its nine-week plan, you would come
away with the truth about who you are, what you want, and where you are
headed. I said you would know what course of action to take in order to have

the life of your dreams. If you followed the pathway I described, you would ultimately be directed to design a clear, concrete, measurable course of action to take you to the top of your dreams, the top of your world, and the top of your life. So, now you are here and you have it—you are ready to pull together all the pieces and complete the blueprint.

As you become clear about your dream life, you are in the position to create a life with an abundance of time, energy, health, and financial reserves. When your life is ideal, the concept of time involves only being in the moment, immersed in peace, joy, contentment, and gratitude; you experience enough silence to hear the voice of your spirit and have plenty of energy to follow your dreams.

You become what you think about all day long and those days become your life.

— Anonymous - from:

EMDR* Seminar Lecture

(*Eye Movement Desensitization Reprogramming)

Tailoring Your Dream Life

Now is time to put all that you love and want together, make it real, and watch it come alive. Have you tailored your dream life, shaped it, and made it your own? This is the time to create specific goals and design the plan for making your desires come true.

This is *not* the time to be practical. By this I mean that when you design your dream life, do not censor anything you desire simply because it is not practical. Let the ideas of your mind, your heart, and your spirit flow without censorship so that they may inform you of their dreams. Life is at your feet just asking you to become clear about what you want. Now is the time to take all that you want and package it to suit your pace and your plan for the future.

Plans and goals must be written and explicit. You must describe them in the smallest of detail. As Steven Covey says: Begin with the end in mind. You must have a clear image in your mind of exactly what your goal is. With each goal you need to:

- write down the steps you are going to take to achieve it.

- create a timeline.

- determine what skills, education or experience you will need to attain your goal, and then put all your focus on gaining it.

With the end in mind, what do you need to do:

- today,

- this week,

- this month,

- this year,

- next year, and on into the future,

to bring you closer to attaining your goal in the time that you have defined. Is it completing college, or doing an internship to gain on the job training? Is it creating a reading list consisting of books and articles to read over a period of time to become an expert in your field? Clearly define what you must do, have, or know in order to create the life you dream of.

I have coached many people who have had the things that mean the most to them begin to show up once they became completely focused, clear, and unwavering in their loyalty to their path, desires, and soul's quest. Jenny Ditzler, author of *Best Year Yet,* states that 80 percent of the goals we write down are attained without even consciously trying to achieve them! Once you have identified your goals, things begin to happen.

Dream the Impossible

If your dream comes from your authentic self it will show up. You will manifest it. This is a time to choose positive self-talk, stay out of your head and go into your heart and your higher self. This is a time to hold the space of trust and faith and then let go.

Are you going to do all the work of this book and then put it down at this "final crux move"? (For those of you who are not mountain climbers, the "final crux move" is the one with which you pull yourself to the top, or in this case, to your goal.) I once had a boyfriend who loved our relationship and was inspired by the way we were together spiritually, intellectually, emotionally, and physically. He cherished the unconditional nature of our love and talked about having dreamed all his life about meeting someone who he perceived was athletic, financially independent, outgoing, intelligent, and playful as well as romantic and sensual. He said that our relationship exceeded all his criteria for an ideal partnership. Later in the relationship he told me that all the things he loved about me had challenged him to step out of his comfort zone. He described himself as a "black and white person," the type of individual who likes to figure everything out and define things neatly. So, for him, I represented growth and change. I made him think he was going to have to take his heart to another level and add some color to his black and white paradigm. Just when he was ready to make his "final crux move," he felt the risk was too great and the uncharted waters too turbulent and he ended the relationship. The risk of opening up to the possibilities of our relationship was truly too overwhelming for him.

"We must walk consciously only part way toward our goal and then leap in the dark to our success."

— Henry David Thoreau

So, will you run away now from this life-altering plan? Will you shrink back as my wonderful friend did? It seems fitting to call this plan the "final crux move." This move has the potential to bring you to the top of one of your spiritual peaks and allow the incredible unfolding of your dream. This step involves your commitment to step into your truth and your power. It's the opportunity to raise the bar and get everything you want in your life. Don't let it overwhelm you. Be true to your core and finish this worthy and challenging process.

The most meaningful thing you can live for is to reach your full potential. At any given age the body and mind you experience are but a fraction of the possibilities still open to you – there are always infinite new skills, insights, and depths of realization ahead of you"

— Deepak Chopra, M.D.

Who am I?

This is the piece of the work you began in Chapter 1. As you write your goals, you may find you need to buff up or revise some of the materials you designed previously. I strongly recommend that you answer the questions in this chapter before you look back at your original answers to these same questions, which you wrote in your journal at the end of Chapter 1. I suggest that you only refer to your original answer after you have written it down this time. The best way to approach this is by closing your eyes for a few minutes, becoming still, or by listening to the Chapter 1 meditation again. Examples of who I am can be:

- I am a strong, compassionate striving warrior.

- I am truth, friendship, wholeness, and knowledge.

- I am dancing, light, playful, abundant energy.

- I am grounded, practical, and on purpose.

Whether your description of who you are is simple or complex is not important. What is important is that your description of yourself has life and meaning to you because then you can trust that your description is right.

What is the most erroneous attitude I have about myself?

In other words, what is the old tale you tell yourself that holds you back? If you remember, we covered this in Chapter 2. What are the words on the broken record that your family, teachers, friends, or coaches started for you that you continue to stick to as if they were true? What limiting messages did you pick up along the way and hold onto and believe as if they are the truth?

What are the biggest limiting beliefs preventing you from having the life you want? List them in your journal. This is the list of "stuff" you say to yourself, the reasons you tell yourself you can't have the dream life. I call them your "limiting thoughts" and they are really the excuses you use to explain why you can't have or even work toward the perfect life.

Now take each negative belief or thought and turn it into a positive. "I am complete" versus "I am not good enough." Turn "I am bad" into "I am awesome." Convert "I can't" into "I can." "This will never happen to me" turns into "I easily manifest, attract, and create my dream life."

Tell yourself, "I deserve my dream life," "I am all it takes to have an abundant life," and "I have the intelligence and discipline it takes to live the great life." These positive statements will be included in the summary at the end of this chapter.

What takes my power?

What takes away your strength and stops you from believing in your dream? I suggest you take a few minutes of silence and close your eyes. Go inside yourself and pull up the aspect of yourself that feeds powerlessness. Ask how this aspect, such as self-doubt, serves you. In other words, what do you receive from the self-doubt? What benefit does it have for you? This may sound silly but see if you can find an answer. Write down what comes to you to examine later, even if it seems inconsequential. The benefit may be to guard you from going out too far on a limb. It may think it is keeping you safe by cautioning you. Write down the answers in your journal. Answer the question: What about this thought or aspect of myself holds me back, and keeps me from being powerful? Some typical examples of things that may take your power include self-doubt, lack of clarity, negative relationships, chaos, anger, fear, or lack of forgiveness. You worked on this in Chapter 7. In the next section you will be required to focus on achieving closure with these demons.

To complete this section you need to come up with a power statement that embodies your commitment to step into your power. Write it in your journal. Examples include:

- I am in my power. I choose a daily practice of forgiveness.

- I am my highest self. I practice clarity.

- I am all that I can and want to be because I am free of self-doubt.

This power statement will be in your summary, but for now, don't worry if you don't believe it. This is one of those "fake it 'til you make it" ideas.

What are my values?

What are the values that drive your life? List in your journal the things that are at the core of your highest authentic self. Some examples include: freedom, acceptance, love, joy, accomplishment, happiness, and intimacy.

Take a few moments and close your eyes. Take a few deep breaths and go back to the place inside you where you feel most connected to yourself and ask, "What are my strongest values?" Don't censor your answer, acknowledge each value as it comes to you and jot down each value. When you have completed this process, go back to the values you wrote down while you were working on Chapter 2 and then again in Chapter 8. How similar or different is this current list of values to the original list of values you wrote? You will know this list of values is authentic if it is resonating with your spirit and if they energize and support your dream life.

What are the top five responsibilities or roles in my life?

What roles do you play? Which role needs the most attention? Roles or responsibilities include such things as daughter, employee, employer, friend, brother, community member, father, mother, housekeeper, breadwinner. Your top five will get the majority of your attention in the next three to six months. Choose the roles you believe will help you make the biggest shift in your life. In other words, when given the attention they need, improving which roles will help you make the biggest leap into the life of your dreams?

What are the top two things I would like to accomplish with each responsibility/role?

Let's say being an employee is one responsibility. You could say, "The top two things I need to do as an employee that will make the biggest difference in the life of my dreams are: to complete all projects two days ahead of deadline and to stay focused."

If your role as a brother is one of your most important, then an example of the two things that will make the biggest difference might be: to make two phone calls a week to the sibling of my choice and to attend one extended family gathering per quarter.

Go ahead now and choose your top roles and identify the two critical actions you can take that will expand your life and move you forward on your path. Record these in your journal.

What are my dreams?

Now is the time to define the dreams you want to fulfill in the following categories: financial, emotional, physical, relational, career, familial, intellectual, spiritual, and any other areas that are important to you. I suggest you plan to take several hours to complete this section. Do the meditation before addressing each category in your journal. This may take several days. Do not judge, doubt or censor your desires as you complete this process. Remember, you are addressing the dreams or goals you want to achieve in each area of your life. Give yourself all the time you need to form your ideal plan for each these important categories.

What needs to be your first priority?

This is the area in which you can experience the biggest advancement toward your dreams—if you make it your focus. Focus on the roles that will make the biggest difference in having the life of your dreams. For example, if you are a single mother, you may say parenting is your number one respon-sibility or role. If this role were given a great deal of attention or focus to improve it, the improvement might create more progress toward your perfect life than working on other less important priorities.

What are the five most significant goals that support your first priority?

With respect to your first priority, what are the five supporting goals that you will focus on for the next three to six months in order to move you closer to your dream. Are these goals supported by your values? If your first priority is financial and one of your values is freedom, then the financial priority must be supported by the value of freedom. For example, if you choose your financial role as your most important responsibility, you give energy to it.

Make the list for each value category. And I suggest that you look at the dream daily to check for any resistance to the idea that you cannot attain your dream goal. You must keep confronting doubt or resistance and consciously let it go or breathe into it until it loses its power. Complete the rest of this exercise with a specific and measurable plan. Your statements may look like:

- I want to make at least _____$ by the end of next year. This financial abundance supports my basic value of freedom. This means that each month I must make _____$ in order to achieve this financial goal. Next I must define the steps I will be taking today, this week, this month, and so forth, to fulfill this goal.

- What do I need to add or subtract from my work life to achieve this goal?

- Do I need to change jobs?

- Do I need to negotiate an increase in salary with my current employer?

- Do I need to change the focus of my energies in my current position?

What do you need to have accomplished by the end of this year, by the end of next year and so on, to have your dream life within five years?

In other words, go five years out and work back to this year—or this month or week. It is often difficult to think about something five years away unless you have a clearly defined picture in your mind of what your goals must be for each of the coming years, and then, month by month and week by week within those years.

Destiny is not a matter of choice. It is not a thing to be waited for, it is a thing to be achieved

Best Year Yet Lecture, September, 2001

— TIM DITZLER

Summary

The ultimate compliment to God is to BE the ultimate you and LIVE your life in the place from which *your* Spirit Dances.

Spirit awaits in ecstasy for you to dance in the light of your perfect life.

— MELANEY SREENAN, PH.D.

Meditation

Go now to the quiet gentle place in your being. Find your breath and take it in full, strong, and powerfully. Feel your body give in to the stillness you have stepped into. Releasing, letting go, more and more into the love, truth and energy within. Slowing, deepening, flowing, drifting, softer, clearer, quieter, gentler. As you reach this place of being still, let all that may be taking your energy or distracting you float away like a cloud across the sky. Drifting, floating. Floating, drifting. Scan your body, mind and spirit for any tension or worry that you might have and let it go. Clear all your mental, physical, spiritual, and emotional space for this next exercise. You are going to go one step deeper now, breathing into the truest highest wisdom you know within and without. Let go. Trust. Breathe in three strong generous breaths and as you breathe out release any fear, resistance or other emotions that may block you. Breathing. Breathing. In and out. Breathing out any unimportant or undesirable emotions, thoughts, concerns. Stepping now into the depth and flow of spirit dances. Becoming even more and more relaxed and aware of the support and love that you feel at this deep dancing spirit level.

Now with all your spirit dancing, connect with your biggest dreams, fantasies, and desires. What are they? Let the images, thoughts and energies flow without reserve, comparison or reason. Embrace the dancing spirit in your being. Let it flow. Dreams, desires, passions, awareness, flowing, growing, building, connecting, becoming real. Hear your heart and soul shout "I am!" Take in the feelings of the dream. Let the spirit of your soul's passion dance around you. Let the feelings fill you with all energy, passion and truth your heart can bear. Breathe into it. Soak up this knowledge, this desire, this heart dream, this spirit dancing like a sponge soaking up water. Absorb every aspect of its wisdom and joy. Breathe into it again, deeper and deeper, and with each breath let it fill you with the confidence to make it happen. Play with the images once again. Make them come alive with belief in your heart's desire. Smile. Soak it up. Cling to the feelings and let them flow within and without.

Stay in this space for awhile. Silent and free. When you are ready, come back to this room bringing with you all the love and life and joy you have experienced *as well as the wisdom and longing you have soaked up. Keep it close to you as you slowly open your eyes. Now take out your journal and answer the questions in the fieldplay below.*

Fieldplay

1. Describe in writing your dream life in detail. Address each important area:

   • Where do you live? Describe the geographic area in which you live. Is it in the mountains, near the ocean, in the city, in a small town, or in the desert?

   • What do all elements of your environment look like? Describe the inside of your home including such things as number of rooms, style of furniture, floor coverings, views from the windows, number of windows, whether it is a house or a condo or some other abode. Be sure to include your dream rooms such as exercise room, office, art studio, workshop, or sauna. Describe the kitchen and bathrooms in detail. Do you have a yard, a deck, a patio, a balcony, a lake, or a garden?

   • What is your work space like? Describe whether it is in your home, in the city, on the road, in other people's homes, outside, huge desk, small desk, alone, secretary, support team, big, medium, or small.

   • What are you like? How do you look? Describe yourself with such words as self-confident, physically fit, at peace, full of joy, loving, kind, compassionate or thoughtful.

   • Who is there with you? Do you have friends, pets and neighbors? Describe who lives with you, who you work with, your friends, your family, your customers, your children, your pets, or your neighbors.

• What is your financial situation? Describe the level of your financial security, how much you earn each year, what type of investments you have, the amount of your savings, or how much your investments earn each year.

• How do you spend your time? Describe the balance of your time among the major categories in your life, such as the amount of time you spend with your family, at work, exercising, vacationing, relaxing, or on hobbies.

• How do you feel in this perfect life? Describe your emotional state with such words as calm, happy, peaceful, grateful, joyous, curious, invigorated, energetic, rested, grounded, playful, loving, or kind.

• What do you do for leisure and entertainment? Do you attend the theatre, go to movies, read books, run the marathon, climb mountains, fish, camp, putter around the house and garden, cook, woodwork, skydive, or travel?

• What gives you fulfillment and joy? Perhaps it is spending time with your family, meditating, closing a big deal, volunteering at the local mission, depositing your huge check in the bank, having the financial resources to help those in need, creating art, reading or a great book.

2. Once you have your dream life written down in detail, condense your description into a daily, readable paragraph or poem. The following are two examples of what a daily poem might look like:

Today I am born anew as one precious child of God. I live and love totally on purpose, serving God and living a miraculous life.

I am born unto a safe, loving, healthy, honest world.

I am born unto myself with all the power God has given me, to go out and proclaim my highest truth and attract complete abundance in every realm.

— MELANEY SREENAN, PH.D.

God's warrior spirit I am without a doubt.
Love and laughter are what life is all about.
Joy and bliss are the key for it's you and me.
Health and wealth abound and nature is everywhere around.
I spread honor and cheer to all who are near.
Every date is a new fresh relate with my mate.
Life is great. Better than first rate.
Horse and dog and tennis too all are grand
with plenty of land and overflowing with love at hand.
For nothing I yearn.
Bliss at every turn and always time to burn.
Attracting complete abundance in every realm with God at the helm.
Every provision is made for my vision, with Higher Self in the lead,
I ride my spirited steed.
He is my guide.
I have so much pride.

— MELANEY SREENAN, PH.D.

Daily Play

1. Once you have put your dream life in readable form, read it daily. Make it come alive by adding music, dancing to it, putting it on tape and

playing it back, or making a collage of it and hanging it on your wall.

2. Believe in and visualize your dream life daily as though it already existed.

Resources

Doing Work You Love: Discovering Your Purpose and Realizing Your Dreams, Cheryl Gilman; NTC Publishing Group, 1997.

This book provides proof that we can create a livelihood for ourselves today that only yesterday would have seemed like an impossible dream.

The Laws of Spirit: A Tale of Transformation, Powerful Truths for Making Life Work, Dan Millman; H.J. Kramer, 1995.

A parable of a wise woman and laws of spirit, which help to make life work smoothly. A gentle reflection and spiritual education for all, the laws of spirit are at the basis of all religious traditions. Millman's outline documents their importance.

Unconditional Life: Discovering the Power to Fulfill Your Dreams, Deepak Chopra; Bantam Books, 1992.

Deepak uses his knowledge of the body and mind to teach the reader how to create a powerful inner life.

Your Best Year Yet!, Jinny S. Ditzler; Time Warner, 2000.

Clear, internationally used system for planning your life and making it happen.

New Age Magazine
www.newage.com
(800) 782-7006

Designed for people who want to live their lives in a more balanced, holistic way. New Age provides resources, information and inspiration to help you stay healthy in mind, body and spirit.

CHAPTER 10

THE BEST OF LIFE

Spirit taught me to dance to the essence my soul's destiny.

— MELANEY SREENAN, PH.D.

There are only two ways to live your life. One is as though nothing is a miracle. The other is as though everything is a miracle.

— ALBERT EINSTEIN

The following is a suggested format and an example for helping you create a summary of the most important elements and characteristics of your "Dream Life Plan":

Dream Life Plan

WHO AM I?

I am a precious, vibrant, passionate warrior spirit of God.

MY ATTITUDE ABOUT MYSELF IS:

I am complete whole and powerful.

MY VALUES ARE:

Freedom, joy, abundance, nature, truth, silence, romance, intimacy, playfulness, passion.

MY POWER STATEMENT IS:

I am joy. I am fearless. I trust myself fully.

TOP FIVE ROLES:

Son; Husband; CEO; Tennis Player; Board Member

FOCUS AND GOAL WITH EACH ROLE:

	FOCUS	GOAL
Son	Call Parents daily.	Visit them weekly.
Husband	Do one thoughtful thing a day.	Have a weekly date.
CEO	Complete strategic plan with team.	Offer acknowledgement daily.
Tennis Player	Practice Tuesday and Thursday for one hour.	Play one tournament monthly.
Board Member	Attend all meetings.	Commit to new focus.

FOCUS FOR EACH AREA and DREAM FOR EACH AREA:

	FOCUS	DREAM
EMOTIONAL	Meditate daily.	Be totally blissful.
FINANCIAL	Create a budget and a financial plan.	Make $350,000 per year effortlessly.
INTELLECTUAL	Read at least one book per month.	Have abundance of intellectual stimulation daily.
RELATIONAL	Treat my partner daily with a one-minute time-out where I completely focus on her.	Have the passion of a lifetime with my mate.
PHYSICAL	Enjoy some outdoor activity twenty minutes every day.	Be the ultimate that I can be in health and well-being.
SPIRITUAL	Each evening spend ten minutes daily listing miracles of the day.	Have a continuous conversation with God.
FAMILY	Daily ask each member of the family describe the happiest moment and most challenging moment of the day.	Growing, open communication, and continuous intention to connect.

MAJOR PRIORITY:

Honoring my highest, spirit-dancing self.

TOP FIVE GOALS FOR THE NEXT THREE MONTHS:

☐ 1. Stay focused on my dream by reading my perfect life vision daily.

☐ 2. Manifest my dreams by sticking to the plan and telling others about it.

☐ 3. Create and stick to the five-year budget plan.

☐ 4. Continue to raise the bar on my health and well-being by getting twenty minutes of exercise a day.

☐ 5. Move to the country this year.

THE DREAM LIFE - A FIVE YEAR PLAN

The following is an example for helping you create a five year "Dream Life Plan" of your own; it includes the goals that you might have for the next three months:

TOP FIVE GOALS FOR THE NEXT THREE MONTHS:

Same as above.

THE THREE TO FIVE YEAR PLAN:

Write a description for each of the items listed under each year.

YEAR FIVE

1. Dream

2. Top Five Responsibilities/Roles

3. Number One Priority you will focus on for the year

    a. This priority will be broken down later as you review your plan every three to six months, and when you arrive at year five you will break it down into three-month increments.

4. Your power statement
5. Top Five Goals to be accomplished

YEAR FOUR

1. Dream
2. Top Five Responsibilities/Roles
3. Number One Priority
4. Your Power Statement
5. Top Five Goals

YEAR THREE

1. Dream
2. Top Five Responsibilities/Roles
3. Number One Priority
4. Your Power Statement
5. Top Five Goals

NEXT YEAR

1. Dream
2. Top Five Responsibilities/Roles
3. Number One Priority
4. Your Power Statement
5. Top Five Goals

THIS YEAR

You have done this year's plan already. I suggest you review it monthly. I revise any goals that need revision monthly as events unfold. I also review the five-year plan monthly just to keep it in the flow of my consciousness and in my heart. Sometimes the Universe gives me things in fast-forward motion. So for example, two goals that I have planned to achieve in three months are, all of a sudden, in front of me now. You must be open to the process of life unfolding before you at lightening speeds and of the goals coming to you as you reach for them. Remember the idea of spirit dancing! This year's plans are the foundation for the years to come, so work, play and dance with them!

Summary

During each moment of this process, I want you to know that I honor, acknowledge, and cherish you for your deep courage and your commitment to the soulful journey you have embarked upon. You remain in my thoughts and forever on my heart as you realize your ultimate self and dance the spirit of *Spirit Dances*.

Spirit dances on the wings of the music of your heart's highest dream.

LOVE, MELANEY

SEMINARS, WORKBOOKS AND CD'S

ARE AVAILABLE TO ACCOMPANY YOU ON YOUR JOURNEY

WITH *SPIRIT DANCES*.

DREAM LIFE PLAN WORKSHEET

WHO AM I?

MY ATTITUDE ABOUT MYSELF IS:

MY VALUES ARE:

MY POWER STATEMENT IS:

TOP FIVE ROLES:

1.

2.

3.

4.

5.

FOCUS AND GOAL WITH EACH ROLE:

FOCUS   GOAL

1.

2.

3.

4.

5.

FOCUS FOR EACH AREA and DREAM FOR EACH AREA:

FOCUS   DREAM

EMOTIONAL:

FINANCIAL:

INTELLECTUAL:

RELATIONAL:

PHYSICAL:

SPIRITUAL:

FAMILY:

MAJOR PRIORITIES

1.

2.

3.

4.

5.

WEEKLY VERSION OF: *THE BEST OF LIFE PLAN.*

This version should be revised weekly and I suggest you post and read it daily.

1. DREAM/VISION

   A one or two sentence summary of your dream life.

2. POWER STATEMENT

   Three sentences combining:

   - Who I am?

   - Attitude about myself?

   - My Power Statement.

3. NUMBER ONE PRIORITY THIS WEEK

4. TOP FIVE GOALS

PERSONAL: (1-5)

BUSINESS: (1-5)

5. DAILY COMMITMENTS

List rituals, habits or other things you need to be sure to do daily.

6. WHAT I LOVE ABOUT MY LIFE NOW.

These are things that you are grateful for or miracles you experience along your journey.

7. INTEGRITY/INTENTION

This is the place where you focus on an area in which you are out of alignment with your highest self. This can be anything from telling the whole truth, even when it is easier to lie, to listing the things you need to do to nurture your spirit this week.